Land Ho!—1620

Model of the Mayflower in Pilgrim Hall, Plymouth, Massachusetts

Land Ho!—1620

A Seaman's Story of the *Mayflower* Her Construction, Her Navigation and Her First Landfall

W. Sears Nickerson

Edited with an Introduction by Delores Bird Carpenter

Michigan State University Press
East Lansing

All Michigan State University Press books are produced on paper which meets the requirements of American National Standard of Information Sciences—Permanence of paper for printed materials ANSI Z39.48-1984.

Michigan State University Press
East Lansing, Michigan 48823-5202

03 02 01 00 99 98 97 1 2 3 4 5 6 7 8 9

Library of Congress Cataloging-in-Publication Data

Nickerson, Warren Sears, 1881-1966.
    Land Ho!—1620: a seaman's story of the *Mayflower*, her construction, her navigation, and her first landfall / W. Sears Nickerson; edited with an intro-duction by Delores Bird Carpenter.
        p.   cm.
Includes bibliographical references.
ISBN 0-87013-465-5 (alk. paper)
    1. *Mayflower* (Ship)   2. Pilgrims (New Plymouth Colony)
3. Massachusetts—History—New Plymouth, 1620-1691.
I. Carpenter, Delores Bird.   II. Title.
F68.N65   1997
910'.9163'109032—dc21   96-51685
                                                   CIP

To the Rainbow Finder

Contents

Illustrations and Maps

Acknowledgments

I t is with sincere appreciation that I acknowledge the many people who assisted in the research and preparation of this manuscript. I am grateful to the daughters of W. Sears Nickerson for permission to prepare his book for reprint: Mary A. Marble, Jean C. Primavera, and Elizabeth W. Eldridge. I am indebted to the staff at the library at Cape Cod Community College who are always eager to help me. Mary Sicchio, Curator of the William Brewster Nickerson Memorial Room at Cape Cod Community College, and Kathleen Kersey in the interlibrary loan department deserve special recognition. Randall Mason from Sturgis Library was helpful, as were Gail Costello at Cotuit Public Library and Cathy Belcher at Edgartown Public Library. Doug Flynn loaned me books from his private library. I am grateful to Marion Rawson Vuilleumier for sharing materials gathered from her experience in conducting *Mayflower* tours in England and for promoting my work by way of her television show, *Books and the World*.

I thank Connie Connell for entering primary material into the computer, for assisting me with proofreading, and for typing the rough draft of the bibliography. Keith William Bull also gave valuable help in assisting me to proofread. Other proofreaders include Bruce Lemoine and Deborah Cochran. I thank Kathleen Malenky Bent who answered my computer questions, especially those that related to indexing. I also thank Dick Northrup, who heads Cape Cod Community College's copy center, for photocopying.

Sandra Rodrigues Carpenter, a historian with a background in European expansion and the Plymouth colony, served as my research assistant, doing much of my "footwork," locating secondary sources that were cited and checking the accuracy of the text against these sources, always furnishing me with a photocopy for my verification. She also sent me many title pages for the formation of the bibliography, typed the preliminary draft of the bibliography, proofed my final draft of the bibliography, and gave valuable criticism to my introduction. She looked for published works on the *Mayflower* since the 1931 publication of Nickerson's book; I repeated her research and came up with identical results. Sandra used the Jones Library and the Five-College Library System in Amherst, Massachusetts but relied primarily on the libraries at the University of Massachusetts and Amherst College. She is indebted to Frederic Keith Carpenter and Aaron Kendall who made library "runs."

E. Carleton Nickerson, President Emeritus of Cape Cod Community College and nephew to W. Sears Nickerson, made so many contributions that were so varied in nature and so broad in scope that it would be impossible to list them all. He read aloud to me for days in proofreading the original text against the reprint, and he was always cheering me along. I am grateful to the staff of Michigan State University Press for their roles in the editing and production of this book.

Editor's Introduction

The Mayflower's 1620 Voyage

Three roads merged to join the route that the *Mayflower* took across the Atlantic Ocean from Plymouth, England to what was to become Plymouth, Massachusetts: that of the Separatists, the Merchant Adventurers, and the master of the ship, Christopher Jones.[1]

The Separatists[2]

During the reign of Queen Elizabeth I of England, the Church of England was established by a religious settlement that grew out of a series of acts, resulting in a compromise between Catholicism and Protestantism. This made some people unhappy. Two dissenting sects that sprang up during this time were the Puritans and the Separatists. The Puritans wished to reform the English Church from within, but the Separatists, also known as Brownists after the founder of the movement, Robert Browne, wanted to break with the Church, a position which was interpreted as disloyalty to the Crown. By 1581, Browne had established a church in Norwich where he asserted that his members, by containing some measure of the Spirit of God, could enjoy equal authority in the conduct of their affairs, even the right to elect their own leaders.

Among the central figures in the Separatist movement in the New World were William Brewster and William Bradford. William Brewster, who matriculated at Peterhouse College, Cambridge, served under Queen Elizabeth's diplomatic service as assistant to William Davison. When the Queen sent Davison to the Tower of London for his part in drawing up the death warrant for Mary Queen of Scots, Brewster returned to Scrooby Manor in Lincolnshire, where his father was "Master of the Queen's Postes." Three years later Brewster succeeded his father as Post Master. James I succeeded Elizabeth in 1603. In 1604 at the Hampton Court Conference, in an attempt to quell the nonconformists, James banned private religious meetings which led, in 1605, to over three-hundred clergymen being relieved of their benefices for failure to honor the regulations established at the Hampton Court Conference. Among these pastors were John Smith and John Robinson under whose influence Brewster came when they continued their Separatist ministry in Gainsborough, about ten miles from Scrooby. In Austerfield, a short distance from Scrooby, lived William Bradford, who was to become the second Governor of the Plymouth Colony, spanning thirty-six years, and author of our best primary source for the Pilgrims, *Of Plimoth Plantation*. Bradford, born in March 1590 and orphaned while he was young, was reared by a grandfather and several uncles. At age seventeen, he moved to Scrooby Manor to become the adopted son of Brewster.

Religious persecution made it imperative that the Separatists flee, but to leave England it was necessary to have the government's permission which would not have been granted to dissenters. The congregation at Scrooby, which was financed by Brewster and met at his Manor, with Richard Clifton as pastor and Brewster as presiding elder, bribed a Dutch sea captain to meet them at Scotia Creek on 15 September 1607, to take them to join the Gainsborough group who had already settled in Amsterdam. The captain immediately secured them below decks and divided their cargo between his crew and himself. He had betrayed them to the authorities who took them to nearby Boston where Brewster and Bradford were jailed for a month at Boston Guildhall. Their second attempt was under another Dutch captain, this time from Killingholme Creek at Immingham in North Lincolnshire. Most of the men made it aboard, but the women and children were captured. The fearful ship captain took to the sea, and riding out a fourteen-day storm, they finally arrived in Amsterdam. Popular opinion forced the authorities to release the women and children and to permit them to join their men in the Netherlands. Amsterdam was not without its religious problems, so the Separatists moved to Leyden where they settled for over eleven years.

Discontentment arose in their Leyden home. Brewster was wanted in England because of the books and pamphlets attacking the established Church that he had printed on his privately owned press in Choir Alley, Leyden, from 1617 to 1619 before its confiscation. Other concerns included disagreements with the Armenians and the Calvinists, the fear of non-Puritan influence from the Dutch children on their children, their poor work opportunities, and their inability to integrate totally into the Dutch community. The only viable option that appeared to some members of the group was to join other immigrants in the New World and to establish their lives there with hopes of spreading the gospel in those distant parts.

The Merchant Adventurers

John Carver and Robert Cushman, deacons in the Leyden church, went to London in 1617 to negotiate with the Virginia Company of London, a commercial enterprise which controlled the colonization and trade in the New World. Their desire to promote the gospel in the New World met with no success since the seven articles of their faith to the Company, signed by Pastor John Robinson and William Brewster, were not adequate to pass the authority of the crown. In 1619, another attempt was made, this time by Cushman and Brewster (who had to flee to escape arrest), but the Virginia Company was suffering internal problems and not able to negotiate. (A patent was eventually granted but not signed until the Pilgrims were within a week of sighting Cape Cod.) Failing in London, they met two failures in negotiations with the New Netherlands Company. Eventually, they would succeed in reaching an agreement with the Merchant Adventurers, made up of London merchants, who were interested in financial promise from the New World. Thomas Weston, a London merchant who represented the Adventurers, suggested that the Adventurers finance the seven-year-joint-stock enterprise with the understanding that at the end of the seven years the capital and the profits would be divided among the backers and that the houses and the land cultivated by the "Planters" would be left to them as their private property. The Planters would work five days for the company and two for themselves. Every Planter, age sixteen and over, would receive one free share of stock worth ten pounds with the option to buy others. The agreement of the eleven articles which had been initialed in Holland was changed by Weston before presenting it in London. He stated that at the end of the seven years the houses and lands would be divided between the Planters and the Adventurers, and he deleted the eleventh article which granted two days for private employment. Most of the negotiations that followed took place in London between Cushman and Weston. Both parties faced difficulties from those they represented. Finally, on 1 July 1620, in desperation, fearful of a total collapse of the plan, Cushman and Weston signed the terms without having reached a compromise.

Master of the Mayflower [3]

Born about 1570 to a mariner, Christopher Jones inherited his father's part in a ship, *Marie Fortune,* when he reached eighteen years of age in 1578. He probably shipped out as a cabin boy at about age twelve. In 1593,

Christopher married Sarah Twitt, the daughter of a shipmaster, Thomas Twitt. They had a son Thomas who died in 1596. On Sarah's death, Christopher married the widow, Josian Thompson Gray, another daughter of a Harwich mariner; by 1618 they had six children.

Jones was recognized by King James I when the King granted a new charter to Harwich and appointed Jones, along with twenty-three other men, to be the first capital burgess, granting him the power for life to elect two members of Parliament. The King, to increase the navy, granted Jones one crown of the double rose for every ton burden of *Josian*, a ship Jones had designed, built, and christened after his wife.

By 1609, Jones was master of the *Mayflower* and quarter owner with Christopher Nichols, Thomas Short, and Robert Child. As her master, in August of 1609 he carried hemp, hats, Spanish salt, hops, vinegar, and Gascon wine to Drontheim, Norway and from Drontheim, tar, deals, and herring.

Around 1610 or 1611, Jones moved to London where there was a monopoly of port trade. He settled with his family at Redriffe, now Rotherhithe, and located a berth for the *Mayflower* at Ratcliffe Mill. In May 1612, her cargo was cloth of various kinds, stockings, iron stubs, pewter, and virginals, bound for Rochelle, France; in May 1614, the cargo from Hamburg consisted of satins, sarsenets, taffeta, and lawns; in January 1615, Gascon and Cognac wines from Rochelle.

It is to this man, Christopher Jones, that the Separatists, represented by Robert Cushman and John Carver, and the Merchant Adventurers, represented by Thomas Weston, presented the patent which was under the name of John Pierce and associates for North Virginia or Hudson's River. They wanted from Jones a good master of a solid ship. We do not know how the paths crossed, nor why Jones accepted the challenge. Perhaps at this stage in his career the adventure lured him to the crossing, one which may have contributed to his death and burial in an unknown grave in St. Mary Rotherhithe on 5 March 1622. Not until 1965 was a plaque erected in the church to note his passing.[4]

Jones's ship was soon to follow as the *Mayflower* was declared in ruins on 26 May 1624. Speculations as to what happened to her remains take one to a barn at Jordans, near Chalfont St. Giles, in Buckinghamshire for her timbers and to the pillars of the Independent Chapel at Abingdon in Berkshire for her masts.

On Their Way

The small group of Separatists traveled by canal boat from Nonnenbrug in Leyden, in July 1620, for Delftshaven to board the *Speedwell*, the sister ship, which sailed on July 22 for Southampton. On 5 August the ships weighed anchor, but 100 miles into the trip they turned back because the *Speedwell*'s Captain Reynolds found her to be leaky. At Dartmouth, four days were spend on the *Speedwell* before their departure. Another 300 miles proved her unseaworthy; there was nothing to do but to sail back to Plymouth, England where the *Speedwell* was abandoned and from whence, on 6 September, the *Mayflower* made a successful break for the New World.

W. Sears Nickerson

Sometimes Fate follows a peculiar path in selecting the chroniclers of her history. An uneducated seaman turned undertaker, confined by his heart trouble, seems an unlikely candidate for a historian. Yet, the *New Bedford Standard Times* in June 1957 reported that an Ormond Beach, Florida man, who had documentary proof that nine of his ancestors were aboard the original *Mayflower* when it made its historic voyage, was keeping a daily progress chart on the then current ocean crossing of *Mayflower II*,[5] the replica of the ship which brought the Pilgrims to America in 1620.

> 'They were a tough bunch,' W. Sears Nickerson said with a faint smile. 'And if you want to know what a Pilgrim looked like, take a look at me.' We did. We saw a tall man with gray hair and searching eyes that seem to scan all horizons. His slender figure and erect carriage make it hard to believe he's 77. And for a brief moment, we saw a Pilgrim standing barefoot on the *Mayflower*'s deck clad only in a short sleeved shirt and walking shorts, which were Nickerson's attire during the interview.

Birth

The outward facts of Nickerson's life are simple. He was born Warren Sears Nickerson, in East Harwich, Massachusetts, 5 December 1880, the youngest in a family of nine boys and three girls.[6] He wrote,

> My father Warren Jensen Nickerson, married Mary Atkins of Chatham, who was the daughter of a deep-water sea captain, Captain Joshua Atkins.[7] They set up housekeeping in the old Enos Rogers house northwest across the swamp from grandfather Nickerson's. Father was a district school-master in those days, 'boardin' 'round' with the parents of his pupils in pro-portion to the number of children they had in school. He taught everything from the ABCs to Navigation, but it was not long before the hungry mouths of his own growing brood outdistanced the meager salary of a country school teacher. He turned to the sea for a living as most Cape Codders were doing at that period and finally joined the cod-fishing fleet which harbored in The Bay. In later years he pioneered in the newly developed cranberry cul-ture and made that his sole occupation. . . .

Nickerson at Sea

Leaving the Bay and his tenth grade education at Orleans High School, Nickerson sailed the Seven Seas for almost twenty years and touched at most of the world's major ports in the days of the square-rigger. That was when one was considered a seafarer only after surviving a six-month apprenticeship on a windjammer's rolling deck. If a novice's stomach survived salt pork and hardtack for half a year, he could call himself a sailor.

Marriage

After his years as a sailor, Nickerson returned to Harwich to become a steeplejack. He chose that occupation and followed it for a couple of years because it was the nearest thing to shinnying up a mast. He decided that when people reach their thirties their ideas should become more settled. He married Donna May Corliss (1893-1973), a young woman from Wolfeboro, New Hampshire, on 1 September 1918. She had been the brightest in her class in Brewster Free Academy and had attended Mount Holyoke on a four-year scholarship to study to become a secondary teacher in Latin and English.

He greatly admired his wife's college education; in turn, she was supportive of his writing. He told one potential publisher, "I will have my wife go over the text and correct my slips in punctuation, paragraphing, as well as general grammatical errors. She is a Mt. Holyoke graduate and a language teacher, while I got my A.B. as able seaman in a school where a split maintopsail was of much more concern than a split infinitive." They had three children: Mary, Jean, and Dorothy.[8] Nickerson also had two children by his first wife, Imogene Howes Small: Mary and Elizabeth.[9]

After his brief career as a steeplejack, Nickerson turned to what he thought would be his life's profession. He took a course at the Massachusetts School of Embalming. He then built a successful undertaking business in Harwich; he took great pride in his work, receiving great satisfaction in making someone look good in death. Nickerson also became involved in community service, serving on his home town Board of Selectmen (city council), was treasurer of the Cape Cod Chamber of Commerce, a director of the Cape Cod Trust Co., and he took part in many local Masonic, civil, and religious affairs. He said one reason for his success at the polls as a Harwich Town official was because half of the voters were named Nickerson: "So how could I be defeated on election day?"

Shortly before 1930, Nickerson had a heart attack, and it was then that the doctor told him he would have to move to a warmer climate, to relieve the strain cold weather placed on his heart. He moved his family to Daytona

Beach. The need for leading a quiet life inspired Nickerson to open a gift shop in 1932. "This venture," says Nickerson, "survived wars, blackouts, depressions and hurricanes, and was one of the few to remain so long in the Main St. section" of the city.[10] He went into retirement 30 September 1952, at age seventy-two.

Research, Writing, and Publications

With much time on his hands after his heart attack, W. Sears Nickerson took up as hobbies the study of genealogy and research into the history of Indians in New England. From this interest in his own genealogy, which was readily traced back to the *Mayflower* coupled with his sea-going knowledge, he wrote *Land Ho! 1620 A Seaman's Story of the* Mayflower *Her Construction. Her Navigation and Her First Landfall*, published in 1931 by Houghton Mifflin Company. Seven hundred and fifty copies were printed. Years later in 1957, Nickerson received recognition for his research on the occasion of a medal, designed and cast by sculptor Berthold Nebel for the Cape Cod Pilgrim Memorial Association, to commemorate the arrival of *Mayflower II* in Provincetown Harbor. Of the 100 medals struck, he received one with a presentation letter, which included the following: "Some of our Directors, who have read your book *Land Ho* refer to it as the most authentic, interesting and best written book on the voyage of the Pilgrims and their life."[11] Nickerson later said of the book: "If I were to ever write it over I could condense it a great deal and give it better continuity. However, I was bed-ridden at the time, and it took me back aboard ship where I could forget my own troubles in trying to solve those of the *Mayflower*." He tried to get the *Reader's Digest* to publish a paper on the first New England Town Meeting, condensed from *Land Ho! 1620*, which was referred to by him as a collector's item. He also told them, "so little of an authentic nature concerning the *Mayflower* and her passengers ever reaches the public eye." As to its accuracy, he referred them to Samuel Eliot Morison of Harvard University[12] and Harry F. Sherman of the General Society of *Mayflower* Descendants, both of whom were familiar with his work. He added that he still held a certificate of seamanship for square-rigged ships. In addition to writing that resulted from his personal genealogical research, his extensive study of Native American genealogy and culture made him an unquestioned authority of the Lower Cape Indians. A Thanksgiving Day 1954 letter to his nephew Josh[13] who was trying to get the Chatham Historical Society to publish his papers on the Lower Cape Cod Indians best describes his work. His summary follows:

> I use the term 'Lower Cape' to signify the terrain from Bass River to Provincetown. I have identified about thirteen hundred Indians by name in

this territory, assembled them into families where possible, and grouped the families into the three Tribes into which they seem naturally to fall, namely The Monomoyicks, The Nawsets, and The Sauquatuckets. What I have learned about each individual is authenticated by references to old deeds, documents, court records, military lists, and the like. Taken as a whole, my Papers give a complete picture of Indian Life on the Lower Cape.

Nickerson, following his own leads, was to finally find a publisher for two of his articles with the Massachusetts Archaeological Society: "The Old Sagamore: Mattaquason of Monomoyick" and "Micah Rafe, Indian Man: Last Full Blood on Lower Cape Cod." A local newspaper, *The Cape Codder*, published many articles by him, and I wrote *Early Encounters Native Americans and Europeans in New England From the Papers of W. Sears Nickerson.*[14]

Editorial Practice

The text of *Land Ho!* is reproduced exactly as is in the 1931 printing except that the footnotes have been changed to endnotes which are placed at the conclusion of each chapter. Any errors found in the text or in the footnotes have been corrected in editorial brackets in the appropriate endnotes. In footnotes where Nickerson has listed a range of pages, I have identified the exact page of the quotation by putting the number of the page in editorial brackets in the appropriate endnotes. The bibliography has been silently modernized for convenience in locating sources in the notes. An introduction by the editor and indexing have been added to the Houghton edition.

NOTES

1. For further information, consult the following secondary sources to which I am indebted. Baker, William A. *The* Mayflower *and Other Colonial Vessels.* Annapolis: Naval Institute Press, 1983. Boast, Mary. *The* Mayflower *and Pilgrim Story: Chapters from Rotherhithe and Southwark.* The Council of the London Borough of Southwark, 1973. Caffrey, Kate. *The* Mayflower. New York: Stein and Day, 1974. Cline, Duane A. "Christopher Jones: Master of the *Mayflower.*" *The* Mayflower *Quarterly.* 61:94 (North Kingstown, R.I.: Narragansett Litho, Ltd.) The General Society of *Mayflower* Descendants, 1995. "The *Mayflower.*" *The* Mayflower *Quarterly.* 61:92-94. The General Society of *Mayflower* Descendants, 1995. DeGering, Etta. *Christopher Jones: Captain of the* Mayflower. New York: David McKay Company, Inc., 1965. Gill, Crispin. Mayflower *Remembered: A History of the Plymouth Pilgrims.* New York: Taplinger Publishing Company, 1970. Hackney, Noel C. L. Mayflower: *Classic*

Ships No 2 Their history and how to model them. London: Patrick Stephens, 1970. Heaton, Vernon. *The* Mayflower. New York City: Mayflower Books, 1980. Hills, Leon Clark. *History and Genealogy of the* Mayflower *Planters and First Comers to Ye Olde Colonie.* Two volumes in one. Baltimore: Genealogical Publishing Co., Inc., 1977. Smith, Henry Justin. *The Master of the* Mayflower. Chicago: Willett, Clark & Co., 1936. Willison, George F. *Saints and Strangers: Being the Lives of the Pilgrim Fathers & Their Families, with Their Friends & Foes.* New York: Reynal & Hitchcock, 1945.

2. I have not addressed other passengers on the *Mayflower* in this introduction as they do not fit into a specific classification, and the story as it is generally celebrated today is that of the Separatists.

3. The skipper of a naval ship was a captain; a merchant ship had a master.

4. On 1 July 1995, a statue, placed in the church's garden, was dedicated to honor Christopher Jones.

5. The *Mayflower II* was built at Brixham in Devon and presented to the American people to be moored at Plimoth Plantation. It was sailed across the Atlantic by a volunteer crew under Captain Alan Villiers.

6. W. Sears Nickerson died in January 1966.

7. Captain Atkins, representative of the sturdy stock from which Nickerson descended, came home empty-handed after the British had taken his ship and set him adrift in an open boat. He brought all his belongings tied up in a red bandanna handkerchief slung over his shoulder. "When great-grandma Mehitable met him at the door of the square-top, he laid the bandanna down at her feet and said: 'Well, Hit, here's all I've got left!' But it took more than a British seventy-four to sink Hit, as he called her. 'Oh, no! Josh!' she said. 'You've still got me!' And in his old Bible which lay open on his knees when he was found dead in his chair was written: 'She was a very comfortable woman to live with.'" *W. Sears Nickerson, The Bay—as I See It* (published by his daughters, 1981), p. 22.

8. Currently, Mary A. Marble, Jean C. Primavera, and Dorothy N. Ross (deceased).

9. Currently, Mary Atkins Nickerson (deceased) and Elizabeth W. Eldridge.

10. The information on Nickerson's occupations and family life come from an article by Ed Fulke entitled "Success Story—1880-1952" (*Daytona News Journal,* 12 October 1952) and from Nickerson's daughter Jean C. Primavera.

11. Among the recipients were President Dwight David Eisenhower, Vice-President Richard Milhous Nixon, Senator Leverett Saltonstall, Senator John F. Kennedy, Senator Edward C. Stone, Queen Elizabeth II of England, Captain Alan Villiers, and the crew of *Mayflower* II.

    The government wrote him in World War II and asked for the war effort for the plates of *Land Ho* which he gave them.

    At Pilgrim Monument at Provincetown on display is an enlarged copy of his fold-out map [included in the back of *Land Ho! 1620*], and little ones are sold as souvenirs.

12. Morison taught American Colonial History at Harvard; he was chair for three years of American History at Oxford and the official naval historian for World War II. He followed the voyages of Columbus in a sailing vessel before writing his famous biography *Admiral of the Ocean Sea.*

13. Joshua A. Nickerson, Sr. (1902-1990) was a Cape businessman, president of Nickerson Lumber Company, and a Cape benefactor as well as the author of *Days to Remember*. The material described in this letter is in the Cape Cod National Seashore, South Wellfleet, Massachusetts.

14. For a much more detailed biographical look at Nickerson, see my introduction in *Early Encounters* (East Lansing: Michigan State University Press, 1994) from which this sketch is taken.

Author's Introduction

*Summer being done, all things stand
upon them with a weatherbeaten face*

William Bradford

All my life, since I was a little boy, I have seen the *Mayflower* in the offing of my imagination, making in toward the shores where I was born. Whether heredity plays any part in this vision I cannot say. Perhaps the little ghosts of my ancestors who were on her decks meander through my kindred brain, and, finding a familiar cell, fill it with memories of other days.

Bit by bit, through a long period of years, the picture has grown. Slowly and carefully, as the *Mayflower* herself must have sounded in, perhaps even a little clumsily, I have gradually narrowed down her position from a vague somewhere off Cape Cod, until at last I can stand in the Lookout Tower of the Nauset Coast Guard Station at Eastham, and see her lifting her stub topsails and rakish lateen jigger up out of the wake of the sunrise of November nine, sixteen hundred and twenty, Old Style.

It is very difficult for me to express in language intelligible to the landsman the processes of reasoning by which I have brought her there. So much of it has to do with soundings and knots and bearings and courses, that it falls naturally into sailor jargon which none but a sailor would understand. On the other hand, no one but a sailor, to whom the language of the sea is as his mother tongue, is at all competent to judge whether or not my nautical reckonings are correct. Therefore, in order that my conclusions may make intelligent reading to both seaman and landsman, and each be able to judge the correctness thereof from his own particular angle, I have steered

1

a sort of middle course between the devil and the deep sea, as you might say, in bringing them to paper.

Much has been written on the landing of the Pilgrims by the antiquarian, the historian, and the poet. So far as I know, no one has ever attempted to tell the story from the viewpoint of the seaman and the navigator. Every writer known to me has dismissed the first land sighted by the *Mayflower* with the ambiguous statement that it was Cape Cod. So it was; but the open ocean side of Cape Cod—the Back Side as the natives know it—is over fifty miles long. It stretches from Long Point, outside Provincetown on the north, to the tip of Monomoy, eight miles south of Chatham, and to the sea-farer is one of the most dangerous strips of coast anywhere in the world. Somewhere along this Back Side the *Mayflower* first raised the land at day-break of the ninth, and somewhere off here she cruised for over forty-eight hours after she made it. It was not until the eleventh, two days and two nights later, that she actually anchored in Provincetown Harbor.

The generally accepted statement that it was Cape Cod she first sighted immediately suggests to a seaman the question, 'What part of the Cape was it?' A fifty-mile stretch of dangerous coast is not a good enough landmark for him to run for. Being something of a sailor myself, I have never been sat-isfied to let it go at that. The purpose of this paper is to show as nearly as possible what particular part of the Cape she first saw, where she was when she made it, and where she spent the ensuing time until she arrived in Provincetown.

The two priceless books known as 'Mourt's Relation' and 'Bradford's History' are the only original sources of information from which any reliable account of the passage over and of the first days on the coast has ever been salvaged. Later writers have placed various constructions on what is found there. In order to approach my subject with an open and unprejudiced mind, I have gone directly to the evidence of the men who wrote these books, and were passengers on the *Mayflower*. The incidents in which they took part during these two days, as recorded in their own words, have been the milestones by which I have traced their wanderings. To fill in the gaps between and to supplement the whole, I have obtained authentic informa-tion from reliable sources concerning conditions which they failed to record. With all this as a basis from which to work, I have made a careful study of what the result would be on the navigation of a ship like the *Mayflower,* and what a clear-headed shipmaster would have done under like circumstances.

Mourt's Relation is the most reliable documentary reference in existence covering the days of which I write. It was set down 'by the several actors themselves' while every incident was still vividly fresh in their minds. This record they sent back to England on the first ship to come out after the *Mayflower*, the Fortune, which sailed for Old England in December of 1621, less than a year after the Pilgrims had established themselves in Plymouth. Any detail which may have been at all doubtful in the minds of the actual writers was unquestionably set right before the manuscript left our shores, by other 'actors' who took an equal part in the events chronicled.

'The History of Plimoth Plantation'—'Bradford's History,' as it is commonly known—comes next as an original source. Mr. William Bradford, its author, was a passenger on the *Mayflower*. In later years, while Governor of Plymouth Colony, he wrote of the happenings in which he had taken an active part, as did the authors of Mourt's Relation, of which he was probably one. Bradford's History is only less valuable than the Relation because of the fact that it was written at a later date, when time may have somewhat dimmed the freshness of the memories; and it has not the value of having been subjected to the friendly constructive criticism which there is little doubt Mourt's Relation received.

The landmarks encountered by the *Mayflower*, the courses she steered, the length of time each course was held, the weather conditions she fell in with, the directions from which she had the wind, and much other pertinent information pertaining to the particular days she spent off back of the Cape, is found between the covers of these two volumes, and under the hands of the men who were there. To fill in the intervals which their relations touch only by inference, it has been necessary to accumulate a large amount of related facts and to analyze them carefully. I have adhered to their old style dating throughout, and have corrected all calculations to that style to avoid confusion. It is a simple matter to bring these dates up to our calendar by setting them ahead ten days.

The United States Coast and Geodetic Survey and the United States Naval Observatory at Washington kindly calculated for me, within a very few minutes, the times of the rising and setting of the sun, the positions and phases of the moon, the periods of flood and ebb tide and direction of the tidal currents, for each day and for every position the *Mayflower* could have occupied from the time she made the land until she finally came to anchor.

By their help I have been able to correct all compass courses and bearings to the local variation of the magnetic needle as of 1620; in fact, to plot each day's work as if I were using the compass of the *Mayflower* to steer by. They have also furnished me with authentic charts of the Cape Cod area showing the exact soundings in the track the *Mayflower* followed, as well as much other valuable information.

All the scientific data have been supplemented by that particular and expert local knowledge of the sea along the Back Side of the Cape, which comes only to the ken of the Shoals fisherman, the Coast Guardsman, and the Lightshipman. Many a quirk of the tidal currents and eccentricity of wind and weather along shore are not recorded elsewhere than in the shrewd minds of these canny specialists of the sea. To them the ocean, the sky, and the shifting dunes, tell their inmost secrets; and the things they sense in their close contact with elemental nature are not given to the pass-er-by to even glimpse. I am especially grateful to Captain George B. Nickerson, of the Nauset Coast Guard Station at Eastham, where it is likely the *Mayflower* first made the land, and to C. M. Tobin, Master of Pollack Lightship No. 110, near whose anchorage off Chatham she probably spent the first night on the coast, for their kindly interest and invaluable assistance in aiding me to solve some very knotty problems of a purely local character having to do with conditions of visibility, and peculiarities of the tidal currents near their particular stations.

My brother, Captain T. Carroll Nickerson, who has sailed these waters daily for the last forty years, and whose general knowledge of the waters off the elbow of the Cape is second to that of no living man, has given me the benefit of his great store of practical knowledge.

I have been particularly fortunate in having the advice and suggestions of my old friend and shipmate, Captain Francis E. Hammond, who for twenty-five years has had an unequaled opportunity to observe in minute detail the workings of the tide and weather conditions along the Back Side of the Cape. In addition to holding a Master Mariner's ticket for any size ship, steam or sail, for any ocean in the world, he is a recognized expert as a local pilot, besides having been born and raised on the Cape.

In order to determine what worth-while information the navigating officer of the *Mayflower* had at hand for guidance after he made the land, I have made a close study of the journals, letters, and maps left by the early voyagers concerning the New England coast. A comparison of these charts and descriptions with those of the Colonial period, and so on down to the more recent ones of the Coast and Geodetic Survey and the topographical maps of the Geologic Survey, together with a checking with descriptions found in the old records of land grants, purchases from the Indians, propriety records, and deeds of transfer and division, has given me a fairly approximate idea of what changes have taken place on the Back Side of the Cape since 1620, and how the land lay at that time.

My good friend Stanley W. Smith, Esq., has placed so much rare and valuable historical and documentary matter at my disposal, not only while I have been making this study, but always, that without his continued help and interest, I doubt if I should ever have embarked on this *Mayflower* voyage at all. His private collection of early Cape Cod documents has no equal.

I have delved into the previous history and subsequent fate of the *Mayflower* and her Captain in order to judge more clearly the capabilities of each, and what they might be expected to do under certain conditions. Along with this, a study of the types of ships of the size and vintage of the Mayflower, how they were rigged and equipped, and what instruments and aids to navigation they carried on their voyages, has been necessary. From this and my own knowledge of square-rigged ships, I can make a fair estimate of what Captain Jones might expect of his ship, what astronomical observations he was able to make in determining her position, and how this would affect his decisions.

In this attempt to get at the probable size, draught, and rig of the *Mayflower,* S. C. GilFillan, of the Museum of Science and Industry of Chicago (the new Rosenwald Museum), and Henry W. Royal, of the Pilgrim Society at Plymouth, Massachusetts, have been especially helpful. Through their kindness I have been able to use the specifications and descriptions of the ship which Mr. R. C. Anderson, of England, used in designing the model of the *Mayflower* now in Pilgrim Hall, than which there is nothing better extant.

My own knowledge of the customs obtaining on old-time sailing ships came first-hand and unadulterated in gaining my A. B. before the mast on a square-rigged, deep-water windjammer—an experience, I dare say, vouchsafed very few Americans of the present generation. Because this early training in things nautical led to my attempting this paper, I may be pardoned this personal allusion. I was born and reared on the shore which first gladdened the eyes of the Pilgrims. I have sailed its waters as boy and man, in everything from a fisherman's dory to an ocean steamship, by night and by day, winter and summer. Every land- and sea-mark encountered by the Master of the *Mayflower,* from the morning he raised the land until he anchored his ship in Provincetown Harbor, has been an open book to me since I can remember.

For these reasons I hope to be able to present some nautical aspects affecting the approach of the *Mayflower* to the Back Side of the Cape which might wholly escape the observation of the landsman, no matter how minute and academic his knowledge of the historical facts, but which are of the utmost importance in any discussion of her position at any time.

Each conclusion at which I have arrived has been subjected to the scrutiny and criticism of that fast diminishing class of master mariners who are thoroughly schooled in the navigation and handling of sailing ships. With the facts on which I have based my deductions spread out in chronological sequence before men of this caliber, who are thoroughly familiar with this particular bit of coast, it is not difficult for them to put themselves into

Captain Jones's position on the deck of the *Mayflower,* and lay down her track very closely.

To them, and to every one else who has contributed in any way to assist me in piloting the *Mayflower* in out of the mists of the mighty Atlantic, I express my deepest appreciation and gratitude.

1

The Voyage

The difficulties and delays which the Pilgrims met with in getting away from England, and the contrary weather they encountered on the passage over, had caused the *Mayflower* to be off Cape Cod on the morning of the ninth of November, sixteen hundred and twenty, instead of farther south toward the Jersey shore as was the original intention. Because of these unforeseen and unavoidable setbacks, the whole expedition was in sore straits—ship, crew, and passengers. This condition of affairs needs to be constantly borne in mind in making any study of their manoeuvres after they made the land.

To bring the reader to that date with the grueling circumstances, which had placed the *Mayflower* there, fresh in his mind, and with a clear understanding of how their desperate condition influenced every thought and action of those on board, I am giving a brief sketch of the passage over, a sort of prologue to the real text of this paper. While it is written in rather a fanciful vein, I can assure you that every incident is either a strictly historical fact, or is carefully thought out in relation to what would have been likely to occur on shipboard under conditions which my study of the subject leads me to believe must have been true, and in which I trust the reader will concur after reading Chapter 2.

Daylight hove up clear over the rim of a slick sea. It flooded with sheer gold the eastern heavens and dimmed the waning quarter of the old moon hanging in mid-sky. Spilling down over a softly undulating ocean, it crept westward until it broke against a lone ship, becalmed, and lazily lifting and listing to the ground swell.

For a moment she stood out weird and spectral, a gray silhouette against the western blur of night. Then every rippling fold of her idle canvas, rhythmically swishing and slapping against chafed spars, became shimmering cloth of gold in the wake of the morning. Slowly lifting her high poop up out of a trough of shadows into the sun, the windowed galleries blazed back in radiance. A weathered scroll across the stern, crusted with salt and be-dimmed by the night's dew, turned to luster under the magic touch and revealed the golden legend: *MAYFLOWER* of LONDON.

A curious old turkey gull dipped out of the west and shrilly kee-yakked his utter astonishment at this apparition of a ship under sail. The drowsy helmsman roused at the sound and swung his helm aport to meet the ruffle of the first morning's cat's-paw of wind. Captain Jones straightened up from leaning over the taffrail and dreaming into the dawn. Back there, where the daylight was coming from, in a little cottage in Rotherhithe in Old England, his goodwife Joan with his little Joan and Christopher, had long since said a morning prayer for their sailor, his ship, and his safe return.

He stretched, as a strong man does, to shake off the lethargy of dreams which come in the night watches. Automatically he walked over and peered down into the binnacle to see if his ship had as yet gathered headway enough to come up to her westward course again. Turning his face ques-tioningly toward the lingering darkness ahead, with chin raised and nostrils distended he drank deep of the freshening breeze. 'Smells like land to me,' he soliloquized, half to himself and half to the helmsman in the steerage.

This was the sixty-fifth consecutive day that the good ship *Mayflower* of London, Christopher Jones, Master, had doggedly edged her southwesterly course out across the Western Ocean toward the Northern Parts of Virginia in America. And before that, there had been those heart-breaking August days when, twice in a month, she had made a start only to be forced to put back because of the leakiness of her little sixty-ton consort *Speedwell*.

Even this had not been all for Captain Christopher Jones. For him, the voyage had begun away back in mid-July, over one hundred days ago, when he had weighed from his home anchorage in the Thames and slipped down to Southampton Water, bringing a small party of the Pilgrims from London, where his ship had been chartered, and some from Essex and the surround-ing country.

Arriving at Southampton on the nineteenth of July, he tied up at the West Quay, took on stores, and awaited the coming of the *Speedwell* from the Low Countries with the major company of the Pilgrim band from the congrega-tion at Leyden.

The *Speedwell* sailed from Delfthaven in Holland about the twenty-sec-ond, and made a quick passage across the Channel, but it was two weeks later before the whole company was distributed and quartered between the two ships in a manner satisfactory to themselves and the desires of the two shipmasters. Many of the leading men of the Leyden company were purposely assigned to the little Speedwell as a matter of policy, so that her master, one Captain Reinold, might be satisfied that his ship, though smaller, would be equally as important a unit in the expedition as her mother ship, the one-hundred-and-eighty-ton *Mayflower.*

Unforeseen difficulties in arranging the final business clearances helped to delay the sailing day, so that it was not until a Saturday, the fifth of August, that the two ships put bravely out to sea for the first time, with a 'faire wind,' as Governor Bradford tells us. Even at this late date the prospects were all to the good for a comfortable midsummer passage across, and an arrival in America in ample season to build winter quarters before cold weather set in.

They were hardly out into the Channel, however, before Captain Reinold of the *Speedwell* began to complain that his ship was leaking badly and that he dare not risk going farther to sea in her until she was repaired. There was nothing for it but to run for Dartmouth, the nearest haven, where, after much loss of time, money, and, what was perhaps more precious than either, of favoring winds, the shipwrights found and repaired a few minor leaks and pronounced her seaworthy again.

This delay used up the greater part of the month of August, and it was Wednesday, the twenty-third, before they made sail from Dartmouth for the second start. Land's End was cleared and the two ships had made a three-hundred-mile offing, when again came the signal of distress from Captain Reinold. This time his ship was in a sinking condition. Robert Cushman, who was a passenger on her, writing to a friend soon after, says that they scarcely thought it possible she could stay afloat another hour.

Back they turned again, this time into Plymouth Harbor, where, after a thorough inspection and overhauling, the *Speedwell* was condemned as unfit for their use. Those of her passengers who could best return home were sent back to London with the leaky ship, and the rest were jammed into the already crowded cabins of the *Mayflower.*

This *Speedwell*, on which the Pilgrims had builded such high hopes, came very near to being the complete undoing of the whole expedition. They had bought and fitted her out in Holland to help transport the company overseas, and had shipped a crew to remain a year in the new country to trade and fish in her for the benefit of the prospective colony. As well as a source of revenue, she would also be an insurance against the new settlement being entirely cut off from the civilized world should unforeseen disaster fall on them in the wilderness.

It caused them 'great discouragemente,' they tell us, and well it might. Aside from the disappointment of seeing what they had reckoned as one of their principal assets turned into worse than a liability on their hands, all this trouble with the *Speedwell* delayed their final start until they fell into the season of westerly gales in crossing over, which dragged out the passage until their water, firewood, and fresh provisions were used up and scurvy had a strangle-hold on them before they got over. When they finally did land, amid ice and snow and with their physical vitality at lowest ebb, they were never able to provide adequate shelter at all that first winter, and the wonder is that no more than half their number paid for it with their lives. What a superb example of morale those men and women left their descendants, when the survivors stood on the hills of Plymouth the next spring, among their dead and dying, and watched the *Mayflower* drop over the horizon homeward bound to Old England, and never a one took passage on her!

It afterwards developed that the *Speedwell*'s chief trouble was in being over-sparred, that is, her masts and rig were too tall and heavy for the stress of ocean weather, in relation to her hull. This caused her to 'work,' as sailors express it, in a sea-way and open her seams. Knowing this and beginning to lose their nerve at the prospect ahead of them, it is quite likely her crew aggravated the *Speedwell*'s weakness by crowding on sail, a trick known to every old sailor. It is a matter of record that, after she was sold and her rig cut down, she proved a seaworthy and profitable ship to her new owners.

So at last, with a 'fine small gale' from the east-northeast, the *Mayflower* cleared from Plymouth alone, on a Wednesday, the sixth of September, and romped out by Land's End once more for the open sea. Sinking Old England over the starboard quarter for the last time, with 'faire winds and weather,' she stood boldly to the westward. But the season of the autumnal equinox was now at hand, line gales came roaring up the North Atlantic, and she was 'mette with many fierce storms, with which ye shipe was shroudly shaken, and her upper works made very leakie: and one of the maine beams in ye midd ships was bowed and craked,' as Bradford describes it.

Although they were now in mid-ocean, there were some who thought the voyage must be given over. Captain Jones was not among these, however. He had been shipmate with the *Mayflower* into the Baltic when screaming northers drove frozen spindrift like shot against her sides, and only her staunchness had brought them through. Many a Biscay gale had they weathered together running cargoes up from the southern wine ports. For a dozen years he had proved her worth, and he knew that she was as sound as a nut below the waterline.

With the help of a great jack-screw brought by the Pilgrims out of Holland, he forced the sprung main beam back into place and securely fished it with timbers. Then, with a post under it braced to the lower deck, he swung her off once more to the westward. Even in normally breezy weather he had to ease her through it under short sail, and in heavy weather the caulking worked out and caused many a wet berth below decks, but by skilful seamanship he had nursed her along up to now.

All in all, it had been a pretty irksome voyage from the start. Unknown to Captain Jones, as to every other navigator of his day, he had been bucking the full strength of the set of the Gulf Stream current almost since leaving the Irish coast. Fresh provisions were a thing of the long past. The last of the firewood was gone. Fresh water was so low in the butts that none could be spared for the women to wash their clothes. One of his crew had sickened and died in mid-ocean. Scurvy, that dread enemy of every early voyager, was showing its hideous symptoms among passengers and crew alike. Only last Monday, the sixth of November, little Billie Butten, Doctor Fuller's servant boy, the first of the Pilgrims to go, had been sorrowfully slid over the side to a lonely ocean grave. One mother had already given birth to a baby boy on this long overdue voyage, and another's time was nearly up. Every westerly now came with the bite of winter in its maw, a worrying reminder of the weakened condition of his ship—and still no land in sight. A lesser seaman than Captain Christopher Jones, or a less determined company than his Pilgrim passengers, would have long since turned tail and made a fair wind of it for the English Channel.

Instead, when yesterday's noon sight, the sixty-fourth day out from Plymouth, had given him a position very near the forty-second parallel of North latitude, which he knew to be that of Cape Cod, he had resolved to head her in west on that parallel and keep her so, the weather being clear, until he made the land.

All night he had slatted and rolled in an oily calm. At midnight when the watch was changed the dipsy lead had shown no bottom at a hundred fathoms. A strip of the fading quarter of the moon rose clear about that time and kept them company until sunrise—a welcome companion through the tedious night hours, with its horns pointing on to the westward.

But now was come the break of a new day, fair and clear, a Thursday, the ninth of November. The indigo blue of the offshore depths had changed to emerald. The breath of the land was in his nostrils. Master's Mate, Clark, who had been to Virginia the year before with a shipload of cattle, thought the signs looked as if they were getting in on to soundings.

It is given to the breed of sailormen to forget the miseries and discomforts of black days at sea in the lure of the promise just over the horizon ahead. As daylight filled the *Mayflower*'s sails with wind and the placid ocean around him with golden light, Captain Jones came back to the work ahead with a snap, perhaps even with a grim smile of joy in the fight he was making.

'Bring her up to her course, Master Clark, as soon as she gets steerageway! Turn-to the watch and heave the lead! Send a man aloft to the maintop lookout!' His orders tumbled out thick and fast. Sleepy sailors crawled out from coils of rigging under the weather rail, rubbing their eyes. The deep-sea lead-line was run forward outside the weather rigging, and the grizzled leadsman took his place outside the mizzen shrouds. Up the main ratlines clattered the half-awake lookout man. The tall ship swung slowly around on her heel to her west course again, under the push of the breeze coming up with the sunrise—and another ship's day had begun on board the *Mayflower*.

The singsong rhythm of the old leadsman's voice as he called the marks and deeps, echoed musically back from top-and sprit-sail in the morning hush. Bits of red and white rag and little strips of leather, marking the depths up to twenty fathoms, zipped through his gnarled but experienced hand. Strands of marline, showing twenty—thirty—forty—fifty fathoms, disappeared into the mysterious blue to the tune of his ritual. Then, suddenly, surprised out of his regular drone, his voice snapped into an excited staccato! 'And bottom at eighty fathoms, sir!' it rang out clear and unmistakable!

Captain Jones's heart jumped at the words. At long last he had got hold of the coast of America, that goal for which he had battled as only a sailor can. But the joy of this announcement had short while to stir his thoughts. From the maintop lookout broke out another and more urgent hail—the most welcome sound that ever falls on sea-weary ears:

'La-a-nd Ho-o!! La-a-nd Ho-o!! Land! Land! La-a-nd Ho!!'

It came like a sequel to the chantying troll of the leadsman's 'eighty fathoms.' It rang through the breathless ship, and quickened every soul on board, from the reverend Elder of the flock to little sea-born Oceanus, who never yet had breathed the air of God's green earth.

'Where away?' yelled Captain Jones as he sprang for a shear-pole and swung himself up into the mizzen rigging to see for himself.

'Two points on the weather bow, sir!' came back the quick response; and as the first level rays of the rising sun struck fair into the loom ahead, there it lay, stretching to north and south as far as the eye could reach.

As if to strike the high hour of victory, the ship's bell chimed out the hour of seven—ding-dong—ding-dong—ding-dong—six bells. Half-dressed men, women, and children crowded up from below and clambered to rail and rigging. Sea-tortured eyes strained through tears of joy toward the promised land that was to be their land, come weal, come woe. In all the beauty of the golden sunrise it lay before them, the answer to their prayers, the land of their desires!

Did these staid Pilgrim fathers of ours shout and dance, sing and pray, or were they silenced by the overpowering solemnity of that ecstatic moment? You know as well as I. Perhaps some song-leader found voice and turned their bursting hearts heavenward on the strains of that never-failing and glorious old anthem of praise and thanksgiving, 'Old Hundredth,' which they had along with them, together with their cradles, and chairs, and Dutch cheeses.[1]

William Bradford, who was one of them on that glad morning, writing of it in after years, tells us that 'they were not a little joyful.' I am sure they were.

These ancestors of ours were an intensely human set of men and women. They were the pick and flower of the whole Separatist congregation, every man a volunteer, chosen because of their youth and their virile strength to be the shock troops, as it were, in storming the citadel of the wilderness. In their veins ran the same blood that courses in ours. They were filled with the same human desires, subject to the same underlying emotions, moved by the same fundamental passions. If, then, we can project ourselves back to that momentous ninth of November morning in the year of our Lord sixteen hundred and twenty, and fit ourselves in spirit into the circumstances surrounding that long-suffering and determined band of exiles, then, and only then, we may perhaps be able to sense a little of how they must have reacted to the sublime ecstasy which flooded their very souls.

Notes

1. The Pilgrims had the Psalter with them, with music. 'Old Hundredth' ('Praise God, from whom all blessings flow'), written for one voice, was in it. The words:
   'Showt to Jehovah al the earth,
   Serv ye Jehovah with gladnes,
   Befor him come with singing mirth,
   Know that Jehovah he God is.'

[See below. "they were not a litle joyfull." Bradford, 93]

2

The Ship

The passage across from England to America has brought us up to the morning of the ninth of November, with a clear realization of the distressing predicament in which the Pilgrims found themselves when they sighted land at Cape Cod.

We are now come to the real nub and purpose of this paper, which is the whereabouts of the *Mayflower* during the succeeding days of the ninth, tenth, and eleventh. In leading up to this point, I have purposely refrained from cluttering the pages with notes and references, although each statement thus far made can be substantiated either by cold fact or reasonable logic.

It would be a physical impossibility to name every authority which I have consulted through a lifetime of study on this subject, to name every person, every document, every ancient map which has contributed its mite to the unraveling of this problem. But in order that no one may imagine that I have gone at it in a superficial or haphazard manner, I have, from now on, endeavored to document any statement which might be open to controversy, except where the body of the text makes such reference to source material obviously unnecessary. In addition, at the end of the paper will be found a bibliography of the more important authorities to which I may not have referred directly in my notes.

I deeply regret my utter lack of academic training, both as a scholar and as a writer. I offer this as an apology for any lack of clearness or brevity, and for grammatical or other errors in the King's English. I hope this will be compensated for by my practical knowledge of ships and the sea, my inborn kinship to the sands of Cape Cod, and my dogged determination to take absolutely nothing but the highest authorities for my guide.

Having thus sketchily 'brought them over ye vast and furious ocean and delivered them from all ye periles thereof,' as Bradford puts it, let us see what sort of a ship this *Mayflower* really was which had brought them thus far. Without a working knowledge of her general build, dimensions, and speed; how she was rigged and equipped, and what sort of officers and crew she was manned with, no navigator would attempt to pilot her in through a given set of circumstances.

There is much interesting and entertaining information available concerning the good ship which landed our Pilgrim ancestors on this continent. As my purpose is to know what sort of a ship I am handling as I bring her on to the coast, I have confined myself mostly to what seems to me pertinent to that knowledge.

It is an almost unbelievable fact that nowhere in either Mourt's Relation nor in the Bradford History do the authors call by name the ship which brought them over. Bradford names the smaller ship which they had to abandon as the *Speedwell*, but it is not until the Division of Land in Plymouth, Massachusetts, in 1623, when 'The Falles of their grounds which came first over in the May-Floure'[1] were allotted, that we are certain what ship it was. Modern research has amply corroborated it.

She was a ship of about one hundred and eighty tons burden, according to Governor Bradford,[2] who ought to know, if anyone did. In speaking of the two ships in which they had arranged to make the voyage he says that a 'smale ship (of some 60 tune)' had been bought in Holland,[3] which was the *Speedwell*; and immediately goes on to say that 'Another was hired at London, of burden about 9. score.' There has been much controversy among learned antiquarians as to what he meant by '9. score.' Following as it does right on the heels of his statement about the '60 tune' of the *Speedwell*, I can see nothing else that he could have meant but nine score, or one hundred and eighty tons, for the *Mayflower*. No doubt the Pilgrims hired her according to tonnage, as was the custom of the day,[4] and we may rest assured that they were careful not to pay for more tons carrying space than they got, while, on the other hand, the master of the ship would see to it that he got a full charter for such a hazardous voyage. I feel confident one hundred and eighty tons burden was the basis she was chartered on, and that before the extra passengers from the *Speedwell* were crowded on board, about two tons space was allotted to each person and his goods.

Mr. R. C. Anderson,[5] of Basset Holt, Southampton, the greatest living authority on her build, who designed the best *Mayflower* model extant, that in Pilgrim Hall, Plymouth, Massachusetts, scaled his model to the dimensions of a ship of about one hundred and eighty tons burden, or two hundred and forty-four gross tonnage. A recent examination of the Port Book of London for the year 1620 before July, shows that 'le *Mayflower* of London,' Christopher Jones, Master, discharged a cargo of wine at that port on the twenty-eighth, twenty-ninth, and thirty-first of January of that year, consisting of 153 'tonnes French wynes,' '4 tonnes redd wyne,' and 16 hogsheads of French wine,[6] making in all a total of 161 tons avoirdupois[7] or thereabouts, a pretty close approximation of Bradford's 'about 9. score.' That there is conclusive proof that 'le *Mayflower* of London,' Christopher Jones, Master, is the same ship which brought the Pilgrims over, I will show presently.

Bradford says the master of the 'biger ship,' meaning the *Mayflower,* was 'caled Mr. Jonas,'[8] which is confirmed in Mourt's Relation which refers to the Captain of the *Mayflower* as 'Master Jones, the Master.'[9] The discovery among the documents at Somerset House, London, England, of the copy of the will of William Mullins,[10] father of the famous Priscilla, the original of which was probably written on board the *Mayflower* in Plymouth Harbor on the twenty-first of February, 1621, having as one of its witnesses 'Christopher Joanes,'[11] leaves little doubt as to what Jones was master of the *Mayflower.* The only other known Jones who could possibly have been eligible was a Thomas Jones, and it has been proved that he was in England in April, 1621, while Christopher Jones was still abroad on the *Mayflower* to New England.[12]

It is evident from the Admiralty Court records, as well as from the London Port Books, that Christopher Jones had been master of the *Mayflower* since 1609, at least. In that year he took her to Drontheim, Norway, running into a terrible gale on the return passage, in which he had to jettison part of his cargo of tar, herring, deals, etc., in order to save his ship.[13] Because of the non-delivery of this part of his cargo, lawsuits arose, and on the fourth of May, 1612, Thomas Thompson, a seaman on the *Mayflower* on the Norway voyage, testified that Jones had been Master of her for 'fower or fyve yeares.'[14] This would date her back to about 1608 and make her twelve years old, at least, in 1620. There are plenty of *Mayflower*s antedating this, many of them answering to the probable description of the Pilgrim *Mayflower,* but none identifying themselves positively with her. Anderson says she may even have been alive in 1588.[15]

The records show that the *Mayflower,* Christopher Jones, Master, was in the Thames at London in 1611 and 1613. In 1616 she was there again, probably with a wine cargo this time,[16] and I have already alluded to her 161-ton cargo of wine delivered there in January of 1620. After discharging this last consignment, she cleared from London for La Rochelle the sixth of March, 1620, and was back with another small wine load by the fifteenth of

May,[17] after which it is likely she lay idle, or was being overhauled and painted, until chartered by the Pilgrims some time previous to the nineteenth of July.[18]

This brief sketch of her career from 1608 to 1620 indicates that in build she was an ordinary pot-bellied merchantman, without much doubt similar in design and rig to the conventional merchant ship of around 1600. She seems to have been getting along some in years, if not already fairly old. Nevertheless, the fact that she was in the wine trade is proof that originally she was well built, and still a well-conditioned ship. The buckling of the main beam on the western passage to America[19] may or may not be attributable to her age, considering the severe drubbing she got on that trip. New ships sometimes buckle, under stress of severe thrashing. After that happened, the seams of her upper works opened up in bad weather and spewed their oakum, causing some wet cabins below decks, but there is nothing whatsoever to show that she was anything but tight as a jug below the water line.

The oft-quoted chance remark of Captain John Smith, in his 'General History of Virginia, New England and the Summer Isles,' that she was a leaking, unwholesome ship, referred to the condition of her upper works after her mishap, rather than to any previous inherent weakness. Leaky, bilgey ships were not tolerated in the Baltic nor in the wine trades, and the *Mayflower's* whole known record points to her seaworthiness and soundness.

With her name assured, her captain's name, her tonnage, and something of her past history known, we can go ahead on her probable build and dimensions. Mr. Anderson, to whom I have already referred, took as his standard, from which to obtain specifications for a conventional merchantman of the *Mayflower's* period and probable type, the dimensions of the one hundred and eighty-two-ton Adventure of Ipswich. The Adventure was used in 1627 to illustrate the results of various methods of tonnage measurements, and she happened to be of approximately the same burden as the *Mayflower.* He finally settled on the following figures for dimensions which would fit the *Mayflower:*

Length of keel, sixty-four feet; greatest beam, twenty-six feet inside the planking; depth from beam to top of keel, eleven feet; length from stem-post to stern-post, ninety feet, which follows the shipwrights' old rule that the total rake of bow and stern should equal the beam. These dimensions give a ship of one hundred and eighty-three tons burden, or two hundred and forty-four gross tonnage, of the regular merchantman design.[20]

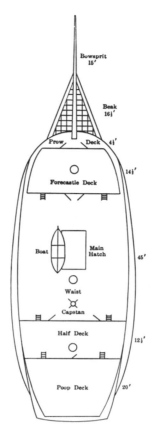

Figure 1. Deck Plan of the *Mayflower*.

We are sure of the *Mayflower*'s tonnage. We know she was a typical merchantman regularly plying in and out of English ports on the established
trade routes. In order to lay down a ship of one hundred and eighty tons
burthen for the merchant marine, certain accepted standards were closely
adhered to by shipwrights of her day. While no specific dimensions directly
applying to the *Mayflower* have ever been unearthed, to my knowledge, it is
safe to assume that if we take the period type of ships of her size and occupation, we must be very nearly correct.

The following approximate measurements apply to a ship of the
Mayflower's size and type, and will give a seaman some idea of what kind of
a ship she was to handle. As I have already stated, there are probably no
actual dimensions of the *Mayflower* herself extant today, and while of
necessity these figures are only approximate, they are based on general rules

followed by shipbuilders at the period when the *Mayflower* was built, to which she must have conformed very closely.

A ship of her type and tonnage was built for roominess and carrying capacity; high-pooped, deep-bellied, able and seaworthy. From the center of the taffrail aft, to the end of the beak under the bowsprit forward, she measured about one hundred and thirteen feet. The bowsprit, which was thirty-six feet long outside the stem-post, extended fifteen feet beyond the beak, giving her a total length over all, from taffrail to tip of bowsprit, of very nearly one hundred and twenty-eight feet, or twice the length of the keel—quite a sizable ship, after all, to swing around in a tight place.

Her greatest beam—that is, twenty-six feet—was very near halfway between stem and stern, and only about a foot and a half above the load-waterline, which coincided very nearly with the level of the gun-deck inside. From this line of greatest width, her sides 'tumbled' in as they went up, so that at the upper deck, or waist, she was only about nineteen feet wide between the tops of the rails. She held her width well forward and aft, however, giving her plenty of deck-room.

The deepest part of her bilge was also amidship, with an easy run aft for leaving the water behind, and a rather flat lift to her bottom forward toward the bluff of her bows; designed rather to slide over the water and crowd it underfoot than to cut it open and force it aside—very much on the principle of the modern sea-sled. This, in my opinion, accounts for her comparatively good sailing qualities when running with a free wind.[21] Her deepest draught was at the extreme after end of her keel, where she drew twelve feet of water when down to the load-waterline, with ten and a half at her forefoot.

The one hundred and thirteen feet of her deck plan was arranged something like this: Forward of the stem-post, which was eleven feet above the load-waterline at the prow, an upturned, pointed beak sixteen and a half feet long and eleven feet wide at its junction with the bow, made a convenient place to handle the spritsail, and an excellent loafing-place for the foremast hands when off watch. Four and a half feet aft of the stem-post was the forward end of the forecastle, which had the upper, or main deck, for its floor and a good six feet of head-room inside. It was fourteen and a half feet long, thirteen feet wide at the forward end and seventeen at its after, and the cook's galley, with range and movable chimney, was in the port side of it. A companion-hatch with stairs led down through its starboard floor to the gun-deck below, and the foremast stepped through its forward end, with the fore-knight back of it. What space was left was given to the crew for quarters, I presume. Two doors, one on the port and one on the starboard side, opened forward to the prow deck, and a set of double doors in a recessed bulkhead opened aft onto the main deck, or waist. Port and starboard ladders led up from the waist to the forecastle deck, which was railed in, and was some fifteen feet above the load-waterline.

Abaft the forecastle was the waist, that part of the upper deck running back to the half-deck. It was forty-five feet long and averaged nearly nineteen feet wide its whole length, with a three-foot-high rail running aft for thirty-two feet and there joining an eight-foot-high bulwarks for the remainder of the distance aft to the half-deck. The lowest dip of the rail was right amidship, just at the point of the greatest width of the deck, where it was eleven feet above load-waterline.

Five and a half feet aft of the forecastle was the main hatch, with a combing rising a foot and a half above the deck planking. It was about nineteen and a half feet long by eight and a half feet wide, and fitted with a grating to give ventilation to the hold below in good weather. The ship's longboat, a craft some twenty-two feet long by seven feet wide, was nested on the port side of the hatch grating.

About a foot aft of the hatch combing stood the main-mast, with the main knight another foot aft of that, leaving fifteen feet of waist clear between it and the half-deck for the upper capstan with its six and a half-foot capstan-bars.

Here the half-deck rose up six and a half feet from the waist, and ran back twelve and a half feet to the break of the poop, with the ship's bell swinging in the belfry on the forward railing. A port and starboard ladder reached it from the waist, and an open railing two and a half feet high on the forward end sloped up to three and a half feet where it met the poop. The mizzen-mast was stepped through the half-deck about eight feet from the forward rail, with the mizzen knight in front of it, and an open hatch through the deck aft of it to the steerage below. This hatch was only a foot long by two and a half feet wide, and served as a speaking-tube through which the navigating officer on deck gave his orders to the man at the helm in the steerage.

The poop deck stepped up another four feet from the half-deck, running back eighteen feet to the taffrail, with side rails slanting up from one and a half feet high at the break to four and a half at the center of the taffrail, away aft. A port and starboard ladder reached it from the half-deck, and between the ladders was a rail across the break.

In other words, the poop and half-deck occupied about one third of the deck space from the stern forward, and the forecastle about one quarter of the deck space from the bow aft.

The stern was nine feet wide at the load-waterline, widening out to sixteen feet at a point six feet above it, and then tapering in again as it went up, until it had narrowed to nine feet at the poop deck, which was about twenty-three feet above the load-waterline. Here, the taffrail stood twenty-seven feet above the water when the ship was loaded, and I have often wondered if this was the spot from which Dorothy Bradford dropped overboard to her death in Provincetown Harbor.

Aside from the necessary pin-rails, cleats, ring-bolts, chocks, etc., which were arranged much as they are on our modern bark-rigged ships, the above sketch gives a general idea of the probable deck plan of the *Mayflower*.

The next deck below was the gun, or lower, deck, where the post was 'set firme in ye lower deck,' as Bradford tells us, to shore up the sprung main beam overhead.[22] It formed the floor of the hold under the upper, or main, deck, described by the Pilgrims as 'betwixt the decks,' where their shallop was stowed in quarters on the passage over, and used as a bed.[23] This hold extended from the bow of the ship seventy-eight feet aft to a bulkhead eight feet forward of the stern, taking in the whole width of the ship, and being about six feet high in the clear. It still goes by the name of 'tween-decks' among sailors, which is probably a hand-me-down from the 'betwixt the decks' of the *Mayflower*'s day.

The foremast stepped through the gun-deck to the stem-post underneath. In front of it was the manger, to catch the water which came in through the hawse-holes on the cables when the anchor was weighed. The bowsprit passed by the starboard side of the foremast and stopped against the main cable bitts back of it.

About amidship, the mainmast stepped through the gun deck to the keel, with a bilge pump on either side of it, and the lower capstan eleven feet abaft it, with a messenger to the main cable. The mizzenmast, which stood six feet forward of the after bulkhead, was stepped to the gun-deck.

Three hatchways opened through the gun-deck to the lower hold, one large cargo hatch just forward of the mainmast, and two smaller ones forward and aft. Four gun-ports opened out through either broadside, and these, with the supporting pillars for the main deck, and the knighthead stanchions, about made up the structure of the 'tween-decks.

Below the gun-deck was the lower hold, running the whole length and breadth of the ship, and averaging from twelve to fourteen feet in depth from gun-deck to keel. Except for the butts of the main and foremasts, there was not an obstacle in the whole length of it, and a large amount of cargo could be stowed away here. I presume there may have been a layer of ballast in the bottom of this hold, covered over with 'dunnage' to stow cargo on.

This brings us to the quarters aft, under the poop and half-decks. The room under the poop deck in the very peak of the stern was the poop house, about sixteen feet long by sixteen at the forward end and twelve aft. It had two windows on each side and a door amidship opening out on to the half-deck. Directly below this was the cabin, thirteen feet long by seventeen at the forward end and thirteen at the after. It had two windows in the stern and one to starboard and port, and starboard and port doors opening forward into the steerage. The steerage, a room twelve feet long by twenty at the forward end and eighteen aft, was directly forward of the cabin, having the main, or upper deck for its floor, and the half-deck for its roof. As its name implies, it was the room where the steering was done. The whipstaff, which took the place of a steering-wheel in those days,[24] came up through rollers in the steerage floor about two feet forward of the after bulkhead, leaving standing room behind it for the steersman. The whipstaff was an upright lever attached to the tiller-head underneath the steerage floor, and here the helmsmen stood their tricks, with light from the little open hatch in the deck above striking down onto the compass in the three-compartment 'bittacle' in front of the whipstaff. Through the little hatch the officer of the deck gave his orders to them and kept an eye on the compass. The mizzenmast stood in front of the binnacle,[25] and in front of that was a companion hatch with steps to the gun-deck below.

Back of the steerage and under the cabin was a little gun-room, with the great tiller swinging through it to the whipstaff. It was eight feet long by nineteen feet forward and thirteen aft, with a gun-port opening out astern on either side of the rudder head, and a door forward on the port side into the 'tween-decks.

She had in all twelve gun-ports, although it is not likely the *Mayflower* carried that many guns. On the gun-deck were stations for eight 'minions,' four to starboard and four to port. The minion was a seven-foot gun carrying a four-pound ball. On the main deck were port and starboard ports for two 'sakers,' a very much lighter and shorter gun. The gun-room under the cabin was designed for two sakers for stern chasers, and the *Mayflower*'s inventory taken in 1624 shows that she also carried 'muskets, arms, pitch-pots and shovels.'[26]

Her rig, as I have stated, was relatively the same as what we know as bark-rigged today; that is, square sails on the fore and main, and fore-and-aft sails on the mizzen. The only difference was that in place of jibs on the bowsprit, there was a square spritsail slung under it, and a latteen or three-cornered sail on the mizzen took the place of the later spanker, or spencer, with gaff and boom. As far as handling and sailing the ship were concerned, these changes made no material difference, and any old sailor familiar with the modern bark would be right at home on the *Mayflower*. I have made a very careful comparison of the arrangement of her sails, and of the standing and running rigging, and I find it differs no more from a little bark on which I served during the last end of the nineteenth century than any other contemporary ship would have done at the time I was going to sea.

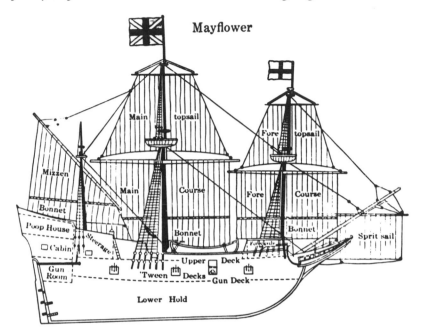

Figure 2. Elevation and Sail Plan of the *Mayflower*

Her mainmast was forty-four feet high above the upper deck, raking aft one foot in thirty, with a twenty-four-foot topmast above the cross-trees, topped by a fourteen-foot staff for the required flag of a merchantman, the 'Union,' with its combined crosses of Saint George and Saint Andrew. The mainyard was fifty feet long, supporting the square mainsail, or main course as the sailors call it, with its forty-five-foot head and twenty-foot leach. A nine-foot 'bonnet' was laced onto the foot of the mainsail in moderate weather, which was easily removed when the wind breezed up, and this device continued in use until well into the latter part of the seventeenth century, when reef points came into use for shortening sail.[27]

The main topsail yard was twenty-three feet long, just about half the length of the mainyard, a rule which was followed until the use of reef points allowed of larger sails and spars. This hung a topsail with a twenty-foot head and a forty-five-foot foot, and about a twenty-eight-foot leach.

The mizzenmast stood thirty-two feet above the half-deck, with a rake aft of one foot in twenty, and a pennant staff eight feet long at its top. Slung diagonally across it was the forty-two-foot yard for the latteen sail corresponding to the modern spanker on American ships. The sail itself was triangular in shape, with about a twenty-five-foot leach and foot, and a six-foot bonnet underneath it.

The foremast, standing thirty feet above the forecastle deck, was topped by nineteen feet of fore topmast, and above that a ten-foot staff for the flag displaying the cross of Saint George. A forty-foot yard crossed the foremast, carrying a square fore course with a thirty-six-foot head and a seventeen-foot leach, and an eight-foot bonnet laced to the foot of it. The eighteen-foot topsail yard hung a fore topsail with a sixteen-foot head, about a twenty-three-foot leach and thirty-six feet on the foot.

Twenty feet out forward of the stem was the spritsail yard, slung under the bowsprit. It was thirty feet long, carrying a square sail twenty-seven feet on the head by fourteen feet deep, which took the place of the modern jibs.

In round numbers, her total spread of canvas, including the bonnets, was very nearly five hundred and twenty-five square yards, divided something like this: seventy-five yards in the latteen mizzen, one hundred and forty-five in the main course, one hundred in the main topsail, one hundred in the fore course, sixty-five in the fore topsail, and forty in the spritsail under the bowsprit.

At the heads of the mainmast and foremast was a circular 'top,' a railed-in standing place for the lookout and for handling the topsails. It was reached by shrouds and ratlines as in modern ships.

A sailor familiar with square-rigged ships will readily see that the *Mayflower* had a well-balanced rig, and would make a very easy handling ship when under way. Jibs had not yet come into use, nor is it likely a small and fairly old merchantman such as she was would have a sprit-topsail over the bowsprit, but the forty-yard spritsail was an exceedingly handy sail in boxing her head around when in stays, or tacking, and was a good puller when running free. Its great disadvantage was that it was under water most of the time when going into a head sea, in spite of the uptilted bowsprit, but the old-timers could always wear ship in an emergency.

The latteen fore-and-aft mizzen was also a great help in spanking her stern around when tacking ship; and when her great main and forecourses, with their bonnets and topsails got drawing in good shape, she would lift along over it as if all the girls in London were pulling the strings.

This rig of the *Mayflower* is not to be sneezed at in the least, and was never improved on very much for a ship of her size and build. While she could not make much headway against head winds, she was not expected to;

and with her high poop and a goose-winged mainsail she would lie hove-to like a duck.

The *Mayflower*'s inventory of 1624 shows that she carried five anchors, probably three spares in addition to the two bowers carried bowsed up to the larboard and starboard fore rigging. The anchors of this period had iron shanks and flukes, but a wooden stock—iron rings for the stocks coming in at a later period. Each bow anchor had a buoy with an eighteen-fathom buoy line attached to it, to prevent losing an anchor in case of being obliged to slip the cable, or parting a hawser while at anchor. These anchor buoys were triced up in the rigging above the anchors when under way, and from the length of the buoy line it is plain they did not figure to anchor in much deeper water than fifteen fathoms.[28]

I have often wondered how and where the hundred-odd passengers were quartered on the *Mayflower*. It has always seemed as if there was scarce room to stow away so many people in addition to the ship's own personnel, and the goods they had to bring along. So I have made a few calculations to see how I should figure it out to accommodate all hands and the cook, were I Master of the *Mayflower*. I may not have this worked out anywhere near right, but at least it is logical and does not crowd them unduly, according to the customs obtaining on early ships.

Of course the first consideration would be to leave ample space so that nothing could interfere with the handling of my ship. Almost as important would be the necessity to keep her in proper trim for a hazardous ocean voyage. With these two prime factors in mind, I should allot the lower hold below the gun-deck for the heaviest goods, especially those which would not have to be broken out until I reached my destination. Of course some of the extra ship stores would be stored here, too.

The 'tween-decks would be given over to the lighter freight, including the provisions for the voyage, and such spare ship stores as would be needed from day to day. Free deck space would have to be left around the gun-ports, the capstan, the bilge-pumps, and all other working parts, and an alley-way fore and aft between the fore-castle and the steerage-companions. I should have in mind that space in the 'tween-decks would also have to be reserved for some of the passengers themselves, but how much would be contingent on how many of them I could accommodate in the after cabins.

Naturally the forecastle, the steerage and the poop house would be the quarters for the crew and officers under normal conditions. With the cook's galley in the port side of the forecastle, there would be no possibility of crowding the foremast hands into smaller quarters than they already had. The steerage, what with the whipstaff, the binnacle, and bunks for the petty

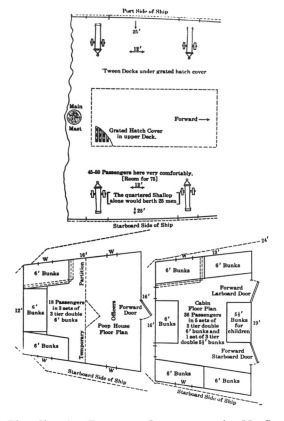

Figure 3. Plan Showing Passenger Quarters on the *Mayflower*

officers and their gear, would be in the same class. The quarters of the
captain and chief officers in the poop house might be cut in half, and it is
quite probable that on such a voyage as this, with its large passenger list,
they would double up and release perhaps half of this house for the use of
the passengers. The cabin, of course, would be free and unencumbered.

I should apportion the rear half of the poop house to the passengers,[29]
and here, with three tiers of double bunks on the starboard side, three on
the port side, and three across the after end, eighteen adult persons could
be accommodated very comfortably, leaving the forward end of the poop
house clear for the officers, so that they might have ready access to the open
deck.

The cabin, with two lengths of double bunks three tiers deep on each
side, a tier across the forward end, and another across the after end, would

furnish quarters for thirty-six more adults, and leave room for them to stir around a bit.

In all, I should figure that I could put around fifty-four grown persons into the rooms aft, and perhaps more if some of the list were little children who could sleep three in a bunk. This would leave a probable forty-five to be provided for in the 'tween-decks.

Naturally, the married couples, the unmarried young women, and the little ones too small to be allowed far from their parents, would be the ones I should select for the quarters aft, where what privacy there was would be theirs. The married men whose wives had not come along, the young unmarried men, and the larger boys could well be segregated in a bunch by themselves in the 'tween-decks.

In going over my passenger list,[30] I should find that there were eighteen married couples, eleven unmarried girls, and eight or ten small children who would have to be kept with their parents or guardians, making in all about fifty-five persons to be given the best choice on accommodations. It is interesting to note that this just about fills the quota of the accommodations in the after houses, and I may add that I figured out the possible space per person before I went over the list to see how many might be expected to be placed there.

I should put the unmarried girls and perhaps one or two of the larger children in the half of the poop house, with three of the married couples with them as supervisors. The little children would go into the cabin with their parents or guardians, along with the other married couples, and this arrangement would take care of all but the married men without their wives, the single men, and the grown boys.

For two very good reasons I should allocate this bunch to the 'tween-decks under the main hatch. The first reason is that here they would have both light and ventilation from the grated hatch overhead. The second is that leaving this space free from cargo would not materially affect the trim of my ship, it being so very nearly amidship. There would also be two gun-ports here on either side for air and light in moderate weather, and this 'tween-deck space has ever been a favorite resort for old deep-water sailors to sling their sleeping-hammocks in.

That this section was used as sleeping-quarters by some of them is certain. The Pilgrims say that their shallop, which they had 'bin forced to cut downe in bestowing her betwixt the decks,' 'was much opened with the peoples lying in her.'[31] Bradford says she was stowed in quarters;[32] and any sailor will agree with me that a large, heavy boat of this sort, even if quartered, would be absolutely certain to be stowed under the main hatch on the gun-deck, both because of ease in handling and to enable her to be broken out the first thing on arrival in America, as she was.[33]

I have no doubt this unit of the passengers made their bunks up in the quarters of the shallop, and on bales of goods and furniture most convenient for their use in this space in the 'tween-decks. The gun-deck was nearly twenty-six feet across from side to side at this point, and twelve feet forward and aft in the clear between the guns, and seventy-five men could be made comfortable here, as men lived aboardship in those days, and still leave plenty of room for a grub table and an alley-way through the cargo to the galley and the cabins aft.[34]

No one will probably ever know just how the Pilgrims jumbled their living quarters on the passage over, but perhaps Captain Jones and the leaders among the company may have figured it out much as I have done, working from the same premises. I have not presumed to speculate on the problem presented by the two visits of the stork, and I imagine this was hardly calculated on by the parties most interested, when the voyage started;[35] but if I were to hazard a guess, I should bet that the Master of the *Mayflower* and his chief officers cleared out from their own quarters so that the old bird would find the best room on the ship ready for him when he arrived.

Her Speed

Judged from any modern standard of speed, the *Mayflower* was a dull sailer. It is twenty-seven hundred and fifty miles from the entrance to the English Channel to Cape Cod,[36] and without any question we can consistently allow her another two hundred and fifty miles for zig-zagging against the contrary winds she assuredly contended with on her western passage. This gives her three thousand miles from land to land, and it took her sixty-five days to make it,[37] or an average speed of about forty-six miles a day. Figured on an hourly basis, she logged a trifle less than two miles per hour, coming over. Taken alone, this would hardly place her in the speed-boat class; but we can be a little charitable when we remember that she was deep loaded, that her bottom must have been extremely foul with grass and barnacles from being in the water all through the hot months,[38] that during the last half of the western passage Captain Jones had to ease up on her every time the wind breezed up, and that she struck right into the season of roaring westerlies. Added to this, all unknown to her skipper, she had been bucking the easterly drift of the Gulf Stream current practically all the way over, which probably set her astern on some days more than she ranged ahead through the water. All in all, it is a wonder she ever got here.

The next spring, in April, she made the homeward passage in about thirty days.[39] Then she was in light sailing trim, however, had the Stream with
her, and the spring westerlies over her shoulder. The deviation from her
course would be appreciably less under these circumstances, and perhaps
one hundred and fifty miles is a safe allowance to add to the true distance.
This gives her a total of twenty-nine hundred miles to the English Channel,
with a daily average of about ninety-six or ninety-seven miles, or just about
four miles per hour with all strings drawing, homeward bound.

Calling the whole round trip out from England and home again fifty-nine
hundred miles—which allows four hundred miles for zigzagging, and is a
very conservative allowance—we get about ninety-five sailing days averaging
a trifle over sixty-two miles a day. This figures down to an hourly sailing
average of about two and a half miles per hour for the whole voyage; and is
probably a very fair representation of what the *Mayflower* could do, taking
it by and large, loaded and in ballast, under varying conditions of wind,
weather, and tidal currents.

Two and a half miles an hour seems a pretty slow gait compared to that
of modern greyhounds. It becomes more interesting, however, when we
compare it with the record made nearly two hundred years later, in perhaps
the greatest deep-water race ever sailed, between the fastest type of sailing
ships every built. At the very zenith of the great clipper-ship era, five crack
tea clippers, the *Taeping*, the *Ariel*, the *Fiery Cross*, the *Taitsing*, and the
Serica, all cleared from Foo Chow, China, within two days of each other, on
the twenty-ninth, thirtieth, and thirty first of May, 1865. Ninety-nine days
later the *Taeping*, the *Ariel*, and the *Serica* docked at London, England, on
the same tide, the *Taitsing* and the *Fiery Cross* only two days behind.[40] We
may rest assured they were driven as few ships before or since have ever been
driven. Their race-course was over sixteen thousand miles long, through
three months of every kind of weather—and the average speed for the whole
course for all three ships was only a fraction over six miles an hour.

During the first ten years of trans-Atlantic service of the famous packet
ships of the Black Ball Line, from 1816 to 1826, an average of forty days for
the westward passage, and of twenty-three for the eastward, was the record,
which was much faster than the average of other fast ships between England
and America at that time,[41] although it averages only around four miles an
hour for the round trip.

In the face of these figures, the little *Mayflower*'s four miles an hour on
her return trip in the spring of 1621, when she got a good break, shows that
she was really a pretty slippery merchantman for her times.

Instruments

Ships of the *Mayflower*'s day carried a very simple outfit of navigating instruments. The compass, the cross-staff or the astrolabe, the log-line with its accompanying sand-glass, parallel rulers and dividers, and a spyglass, about made up the complement for deep-water, or offshore work. On soundings—that is, near enough to the coast to be within a depth of one hundred fathoms or thereabouts—the leadline was the humble but dependable helpmeet.[42]

The compass, for all practical purposes, was the same then as now. The local variation of its magnetic needle from true north, as indicated by the North Star or the meridian altitude of the sun, was a constant source of mystery and anxiety. They soon discovered that the declination was never twice alike in the same place. In the year 1605 it was 18° 40′ west at Nauset.[43] In 1620, the year in which the *Mayflower* arrived, it had shrunk to 13° 40′. From then it waned to 6° 50′ in 1780, since which time it has again been on the increase, until in 1929 it has waxed to 15° 30′ west, or 1° 50′ more than it was in 1620.[44] As previously stated, I have corrected the present declination to that of 1620, so that all courses and bearings given in this paper are the same as were shown by the compass of the *Mayflower*, as nearly as possible.

Whether the *Mayflower* was equipped with the venerable cross-staff for shooting the sun, or with the more up-to-date astrolabe, is open to question. While the astrolabe had been in use for a century or more, it was expensive, complicated, and exceedingly delicate to manipulate, so the merchant captains stuck to their old 'hog-yoke,' as our fathers had a way of calling the cross-staff. We know that Champlain, whose expeditions were well-sponsored and outfitted, used an astrolabe both on shipboard and ashore for making astronomical observations, because he lost his on his 1613 excursion up the Ottawa River, where it came to light in 1867, in what is now the township of Ross, Fairfax County, Ottawa.[45] It is probable, however, that Captain Jones, being a plain merchant skipper, depended on his homely but efficient hog-yoke, which gave as accurate results with much less trouble.

The cross-staff consisted of a graduated staff about thirty-six inches long, across which at right angles was attached a sliding bar about twenty-six inches long. On one end of the staff and on both ends of the bar were sights, so that the observer, holding the sighted end of the staff to his eye, could slide the bar along in a vertical position until the horizon could be seen through the sight on the lower end of the bar, while the heavenly body being observed showed through the sight at the upper end. Thus the angle between the horizon and the heavenly body was obtained with some degree of accuracy, if the ship's deck was not too uneasy underfoot. By the aid of data which had been accumulating since the days of Prince Henry the Navigator, a very close approximation of the latitude north or south of the Equator was possible by this means. Occasionally the North Star was used, but the sun was the old standby.

Longitude was another matter. Those highly developed time-pieces known as chronometers, by which the modern navigator is enabled to determine his distance east or west of Greenwich meridian with a great degree of accuracy, had not then been perfected. Dead reckoning—that is, calculating a ship's easting or westing by the courses steered and the distance run—was the common method. At best it was a matter of good guessing. With head winds and bad weather, aggravated by unknown ocean currents like the Gulf Stream, it was liable to serious error.

Before it was discovered that the declination of the magnetic needle was a constantly changing variable in different localities on the American Coast, attempts were made to determine the longitude by the degree of the needle's variation,[46] but of course this proved unworkable.

With clear weather to get a noon sight of the sun, the old-timers were pretty sure of their latitude, but off soundings their longitude was a nightmare. Captain Jones probably knew within a few miles what degree of north latitude he was on, but I doubt if he could possibly have known his meridian of westing by several hundred miles. No doubt he recognized and made allowance for this.

The log-line and log-glass were the ship's speedometer. The log was originally just that, a log of wood with a line made fast midway of its length, so that, when dropped over the stern of a moving vessel, it immediately took up a position practically stationary in the water, broadside to the course of the ship, causing the line to pay out over the taffrail as the ship ran on away from it. In the *Mayflower*'s day the log had evolved into a quadrant of wood, weighted on one side, having a log-line one hundred and fifty fathoms long and graduated into lengths by short pieces of knotted marline inserted through its strands. Each length, or 'knot,' bore the same relation to the nautical mile of about six thousand and eighty feet as the log-glass did to the conventional hour-glass, and the number of knots run out while the sands of the glass were running through determined the miles, or knots, per hour the ship was logging. Like the old hog-yoke, it was pretty good in fair weather, but in heavy weather and head winds there was considerable slip.

The dividers and parallel rulers, of course, imply maps and charts on which to use them. Captain John Smith summed up the map situation of the English navigators of that period very neatly in his description of his voyage of 1614 to New England. He says that he had with him several plots of 'those Northern parts' so differing from one another, and from any true resemblance to the country, that they did him no more good than so much waste paper, though they cost him more.[47] It seems evident from this that he did not have the French maps made by Champlain and Lescarbot years before; nor is it likely that anyone on the *Mayflower* had ever seen them.

Captain Jones had the description and map which was already in print of the above voyage of Captain Smith,[48] but the map as originally published gave no information concerning the conditions on the Back Side of Cape Cod. Smith only sailed as far south as the tip of the Cape, and took the word of the Indians for what lay to the southward of it, and his original map indicates as much.[49] The old Dutch trade-route from the Low Countries to the trading-post at Manhattan had skirted the Shoals of Cape Cod for many years, but the Hollanders guarded their trade secrets pretty carefully. However, from the long sojourn of the Pilgrims in the Low Countries, and the high esteem with which they were regarded by the Dutch, they may have gained some knowledge of the Atlantic Coast from them, and perhaps seen the Dutch charts[50] of the vicinity for which they were heading. The Pilgrims were also familiar with the experiences of Gosnold, and probably with much other vague and meager information, but if they had had everything that had ever been published, the tangible knowledge to be gained from it all would have been of very little value to Captain Jones when he found himself on the Back Side of the Cape.[51] It was not until nearly two centuries had elapsed that the region around the Shoals was mapped with any degree of accuracy.

When the early shipmaster had any suspicion that his craft was nearing the coast, the deep-sea lead came into immediate use. The 'dipsy' lead, as he called it, weighed from forty to around one hundred pounds, and its line usually was one hundred fathoms, or six hundred feet long. When he got bottom at that depth, he was 'on soundings,' and from there in to the land the leadsman was a very busy man. The old-fashioned deep-water captain hated shoal water as the Devil is reputed to hate holy water, and when the leadline showed he was getting in to anywhere nearer than one hundred fathoms, he was more nervous than if a typhoon threatened him in mid-ocean. At twenty fathoms a seven to fourteen pound lead, called the 'hand-lead,' was substituted for the dipsy, and after that the 'old man' neither slept nor ate until he got his mud-hook down in some safe harbor.

The lead was greased or soaped on the lower end so that the sand or mud would adhere and reveal what kind of bottom it touched. Tradition has it that some Cape Cod skippers could tell by tasting this sample of the bottom what part of the coast they were on. The lead-line was marked off at intervals beginning at two fathoms depth, each 'mark' tricked out with a white rag, a red rag, a strip of leather, or a knotted marline. I can testify that the musical sing-song of an old-time leadsman taking soundings on a quiet night, as the 'marks' and 'deeps' slipped through his experienced hand, was a haunting melody.

This crude but practical equipment includes about everything that the average merchantman of the early seventeenth century had to aid him. It is likely that Captain Jones had little more. With this outfit these ancient master mariners took their little ships across unknown seas to unexplored and uncharted coasts. And what is more, they brought them home again. They were men of keen intelligence, shrewd judgment, and bold courage, and as such no one doffs his hat to their memory quicker than the man who has himself been down to the sea in ships.

Personnel

Master Christopher Jones was of Redriffe, otherwise Rotherhithe, Surrey, England, when he chartered his ship to the Pilgrims. Evidently he had been living there for some time, as his son Christopher was baptized there on the thirteenth of March, 1614, and his little girl Joan on the twenty-sixth of December, 1615, according to the Rotherhithe Parish Registers.[52] He had been master of ships for the past fourteen years at least, first of the *Josan*, or *Jason*, trading to Bordeaux in 1606 or 1607,[53] and since that time in various trades in the *Mayflower*. It is probable he had also been in the Greenland whale fisheries fleet at some time, from what he and his men said about the whales they saw at the Cape,[54] but in what ship it is not known.

His whole record on the Admiralty books shows that he was a shrewd and square business man, as well as a capable sailing master. He owned one quarter of the *Mayflower*,[55] which gave him an added incentive to prosecute his voyages successfully. His chief officer, Master's Mate Clark, had been across to America before, as had also Master's Mate Coppin, who was probably transferred from the *Speedwell* to the *Mayflower* when the *Speedwell* was sent back to London.[56] One of the seamen had been to Newfoundland,[57] but there is nothing to indicate that Captain Jones himself had ever been on the American Coast.

His crew was undoubtedly a pretty tough lot. Any sailor who would ship before the mast for a trans-Atlantic voyage such as this, would hardly be a mollycoddle green hand. Bradford says that they cursed, and they threatened, and they grumbled;[58] but there is an old forecastle maxim which runs, 'Growl ye may, but go ye must'; and any old sailor will bear me out that growling has ever been one of the prerogatives of a foremast-hand. I seriously doubt if they ever were dangerously near to overrunning the authority of such a seasoned skipper as Christopher Jones, or even that they were such a desperate gang of cutthroats as they have been pictured by writers wholly unfamiliar with old-time sailormen.

This bunch was probably not much harder-boiled than the general run of deckhands which Master Jones had been handling all his life. He was right in his prime; and down to within the memory of men now living, the master of a deep-water ship gained his position as much by stark physical superiority as by mental ability, and held it by the same token. His past record shows that he was a bold as well as a skilful seaman, and there is little doubt he was as well able to handle his ship's complement of men as he was the ship herself.

At least one of the crew deserves an appreciative thought from us, for had not 'a lusty seaman which steered' proved the best man in the boat when the Third Exploring Expedition came so near to being lost with their shallop while entering Plymouth Harbor,[59] the story of the Plymouth Colony might be different. Whatever their sins, they paid a dear sacrifice, for almost half their number, including the gunner, boatswain, three quarter-masters, and the cook, lie buried in New England soil with the victims of that sad winter.[60]

The Pilgrim Fathers show nothing but respect and confidence in their allusions to Master Christopher Jones. His was an extremely difficult task; and although he never succeeded in landing them at their objective, in the neighborhood of the Jersey coast, there is nothing to show but that his passengers were fully satisfied that under the circumstances he had done everything humanly possible to reach that goal. No litigation ever arose over the voyage, and they parted in the spring on the best of terms.[61]

I feel that every *Mayflower* descendant, I might say every thoughtful American, owes a deep tribute of respect to the memory of the Master of the *Mayflower*. He made possible the landing of the Pilgrims on our shores, an event without which our national tradition would be immeasurably poorer. His indomitable courage and consummate seamanship overcame every obstacle until he had got his anchor fast in American waters. He paid for it with his life. As far as has ever been learned, this voyage proved his last. The terrible hardships of the winter spent in New England, coupled with the inroads of the scurvy into his system, did for him as it had for fifty per cent of his crew and passengers.

Almost ten months to a day after his arrival home in Old England,[62] he was buried in the churchyard of Rotherhithe, on the fifth of March, 1622, leaving a wife Joan, and two little children to mourn his going. The daughter Joan married Nathaniel Newbury on the twentieth of May, 1636,[63] but what became of the boy Christopher I do not know.

The Prerogative Court books at Somerset House show that on the twenty-sixth of August, 1622, administration was granted on Master Jones's estate to the widow Joan; and on March 4, 1624, the *Mayflower*, which apparently had been lying idle in the Thames since her master's death, was appraised for Robert Childe, John Moore, and Joan Jones, the widow, these three then owning three quarters of the ship. Her appraised value is given as fifty pounds for the hull, twenty-five pounds for five anchors, fifteen pounds for one suit of worn sails, thirty-five pounds for cables, hawsers, and standing rigging, three pounds eight shillings for muskets, arms, pitch-pots, and ten shovels and other items, making a total of one hundred and sixty pounds.[64] How much would she be worth today?

The subsequent fate of the *Mayflower* is not certainly known. She may have been the *Mayflower* which the Dunkirkers captured in 1626. It is certain she was not the *Mayflower* which brought the Higginson party to Salem in 1629; nor the one which was in the Winthrop fleet in 1630, as has often been quoted. At least three other *Mayflowers* made the trip to America before 1650,[65] but after the appraisal of the Pilgrim ship in the Thames, in 1624, she drops out of the picture she did so much to place on the canvas.

Notes

1. *Records of the Colony of New Plymouth,* vol. 12, State ed., 1861. [ouer]
2. *Bradford History,* 72, State ed., 1898.
3. Ibid., 71.
4. This was the basis on which the Earl of Southampton hired ships for the Virginia Company that year. See London Port Books, Bundle 24, No. 3, as quoted by Mr. J. R. Hutchinson, of Clifford's Inn, London, in *New England Historical and Genealogical Register,* 70:337-42. [341] Referred to hereafter as 'Hutchinson.' (Reprinted, in *The* Mayflower *Descendant,* 22:72.)
5. See his article in *Mariners' Mirror,* 2:260-63. Referred to hereafter as 'Anderson.' Vice-President of Society for Nautical Research, England. [vol. 12]
6. Port Book, 24/3 London, examination made at the request of G. Andrews Moriarty, Jr. See *New England Historical and Genealogical Register,* 83:250, 251.
7. 'The liquid ton is equal in weight, or very nearly so, to a ton avoirdupois.' See 'The "Mayflower," Her Identity and Tonnage,' by J. R. Hutchinson, of Clifford's Inn, London, England, *New England Historical and Genealogical Register,* 70:337-42. [The liquid tun, again, is equal in weight, or very nearly equal, to a ton avoirdupois. 341]
8. Bradford, 83, etc.

9. Mourt, 15. [mafter Iones, the Mafter]
10. 'The "Mayflower,"' by R. G. Marsden, in the *English Historical Review,* October, 1904; reprinted in *The* Mayflower *Descendant,* 18:1-13. [13]
11. *The* Mayflower *Descendant,* I:230. Mr. Mullins died on this date, and the certified copy of the will was dated '2: April 1621.'
12. Marsden, see note 10 above.
13. Marsden; also Hutchinson; see note 7 above.
14. Hutchinson, *New England Historical and Genealogical Register,* 70:337-42. [338]
15. Anderson, *Mariners' Mirror,* 2:260-63. [vol. 12]
16. Marsden, *The* Mayflower *Descendant,* 18:I-13. [9]
17. Hutchinson, note 7 above.
18. Marsden, note 16 above. She had arrived in Southampton the nineteenth.
19. Bradford, 92.
20. I am particularly indebted to S. C. GilFillan, A.M., Curator for Social Sciences at the Museum of Science and Industry, Chicago (the new Rosenwald Museum), for his helpfulness in sending me descriptive matter and prints of Mr. Anderson's model; and also to Mr. Henry W. Royal, of the Pilgrim Society, Plymouth, Massachusetts, for furnishing me with the specifications, sail plan, and other data. ["was used in 1627 to illustrate the results of various methods of tonnage" is exactly from Anderson's article "A 'Mayflower' Model," p. 260; Nickerson is also indebted to Anderson for the measurements.]
21. See pp. 28-29, *post.*
22. Bradford, 92.
23. Ibid., 97. Mourt, 12. [Mourt, *Mourt's Relation,* 11.]
24. The steering-wheel did not come into use until about 1700.
25. I have early documents in my possession, *circa* 1700, in which the binnacle is still referred to as the 'bidacle.'
26. See p. 35, *post.*
27. The bonnet is still in use on fishing-schooners' jibs.
28. See p. 75, *post.*
29. See p. 26 for sketch of passenger space.
30. See Bradford's list, *History,* 531-34.
31. Mourt, 11, 12.
32. Bradford, 97.
33. Ibid., 97. Mourt, II.
34 See p. 26 for poop house, cabin, and 'tween-deck space for passengers, drawn to scale.
35. They probably expected to be across long before his arrival.
36. Coast and Geodetic Survey calculation.
37. Mourt, I, 2. She left Plymouth, England, September 6, 1620, and sighted Cape Cod November 9, 1620.
38. She certainly could not have been cleaned since the 19th of July. See note 18 above.

39. She sailed about the 5th of April, 1621, from Plymouth, Massachusetts, and arrived home the 5th or 6th of May, according to Marsden. (See *The* Mayflower *Descendant,* 18:1-13.) [5] She certainly was still in Plymouth when the copy of Mr. Mullin's will was made, April 2, 1621. See note 11 above.

40. *Ships of the Seven Seas,* by Hawthorne Daniel. [70]

41. Ibid. [61]

42. For the list of instruments in common use at this period, and the facts concerning them, I am chiefly indebted to the Coast and Geodetic Survey; *Ships of the Seven Seas,* by Hawthorne Daniel; *Sailing Ships and their Story,* by E. Keble Chatterton; *Elements of Navigation,* by W. J. Henderson; *Ancient and Modern Ships,* by G. C. V. Holmes; and many other sources.

43. *Voyages of Sieur de Champlain,* Prince ed., 2:80, 81. [81, text, and note 167]

44. Calculation of the Coast and Geodetic Survey.

45. *France and New England,* State Street Trust Company Publications, III.

46. Champlain describes this method, and points out its faults in his Voyages. [Prince Society Ed., 3:219-24][County of Renfrew, Ontario, Canada, on his expedition up the Ottawa River in June 1613, and recovered in 1867.]

47. *A Description of New England,* etc., by Captain John Smith. Veazie, 1865, p. 23. [22 and 23]

48. The repeated references in both Mourt and Bradford, to points designated by Smith, make this certain.

49. Map published with the *Description.* See note 47 above.

50. See the Dutch version of Smith's map, and others.

51. I have studied most of the worth-while charts from 1500 down, and I heartily agree with Captain Smith about them, with the exception of the French.

52. Hutchinson, *New England Historical and Genealogical Register,* 70.337-42. [340]

53. Marsden, *The* Mayflower *Descendant,* 18:1-13. [7]

54. Mourt, 4.

55. Marsden, *The* Mayflower *Descendant,* 18:1-13. [10]

56. Bradford, 104; Mourt, 41, 45.

57. Bradford, 102; Mourt, 51.

58. Bradford, 90, 91, 112, 114.

59. Ibid., 105.

60. Bradford, 112.

61. Ibid., 112, 120, 121.

62. The *Mayflower* arrived in England May 5 or 6, 1621. Marsden, *The* Mayflower *Descendant,* 18:1-13. [10]

63. Rotherhithe Parish Registers, Hutchinson, *New England Historical and Genealogical Register,* 70:337-342. [340]

64. Marsden, *The* Mayflower *Descendant,* 18:1-13. [11]

65. Ibid. [3]

3

The Back Side of Cape Cod

The whole answer to the problem of where the *Mayflower* first saw the land, and where she spent her time afterward, hinges on the position she had reached when she turned about and headed back for Provincetown. As the coast lies today, it is obvious to any seaman that a competent shipmaster bound south by Cape Cod would meet with no serious obstacle until he had passed Chatham and came on to the Shoals of Pollack Rip. If the same was true of 1620, then the Shoals become the Rosetta Stone, as it were, making the language of the fathers intelligible to the navigator of today.

These Shoals of Pollack Rip are known as 'The Shoals' in the mother tongue, as no other sandbars on the Back Side, from Long Point to Monomoy Point, have ever risen to that eminence in the estimation of any Cape-Codder. Broadly speaking, they comprise that barrier of shifting, scarcely submerged sandbars lying off easterly from Monomoy Point, and almost blocking the entrance to Nantucket Sound. They begin about seven or eight miles southeasterly from Chatham, and, roughly, embrace the group designated on the latest Coast and Geodetic Survey charts as Bearse's Shoal, Broken Part of Pollack Rip, Pollack Rip, Twelve Foot Shoal, Broken Rip, Great Round Shoal, Little Round Shoal, and the Stone Horse.

In order to arrive at any intelligent estimation of how the land lay on the Back Side in 1620, and determine what changes have taken place there since that time, it is necessary to begin with a general understanding of the peculiar geologic formation and the consequent constant changes because of the action of the winds and the sea.

With this geologic information as a background, I have made a painstaking study of the maps and descriptions left by the early voyagers in the vicinity, compared the results with the maps of the Colonial period, and checked the whole with ancient landmarks long since forgotten, found only in the musty old records of Indian purchase boundaries, land grant locations, ranges in the deeds of the pioneer settlers, and old propriety shares and divisions. A comparison has also been made with the bearings and descriptions set forth in such a practical manner in the early editions of various 'Coast Pilots,' which may be followed down to the present day, and with the 'Reports' of the Harbor and the Province Land Commissioners. Last of all, the net result of all these gleanings has been placed alongside the latest maps of the Coast and Geodetic, the Topographic, and the Geologic Surveys, for comparison with the accurate data of today.

My own intimate observations of the general tendencies governing this shifting shore-line, covering the whole period of my life, coupled with information gathered from old men whose memories and contacts reach back for half a century, and more, before I was born, have been of no little value in helping me to piece the whole fabric together.

From all this I feel that I have attained to a fairly approximate visualization of the Back Side as it was three hundred years ago—at least, so far as it would affect materially the navigation of the *Mayflower.* The large map embodies the main features of this research, showing the probable track of the *Mayflower* in relation to them.

The Back Side of the Cape has undergone great changes since the last glacier left its sands dumped in desolate isolation on top of the old clay beds beneath. Islands have disappeared; harbors have been made and then filled in again; headlands have been laid low and carried north and south to build new land. From High Head in Truro to Nauset Harbor in Eastham the conditions of wear and drift are such that the shore-line is constantly working westward and inland a little. North of Truro the Province lands have made out into deep water a distance of seven miles and more, built solely from the accumulation of this drift. Outside the ancient harbors of Nauset and old Monomoyick Bay another rampart of sand has pushed southward from Eastham to Chatham, and so on for seven miles farther into the ocean toward Nantucket.

Lying off about three miles from the shore-line of today is the 'Edge,' as the fishermen call it, carrying a depth of around twenty fathoms from north of High Head to about opposite Chatham. Outside this twenty-fathom curve, the ocean floor drops down more or less abruptly to a depth of fifty and a hundred fathoms, and deeper. Its curves conform very nearly to those of the coast, even bending in a little closer where the ancient harbors once made in.

While this edge may have worked offshore a little through the backwash from the crumbling shore-front, the known action of the drift alongshore is such as to make this gain appear very slight. There is little indication that any appreciable change is taking place in the relative levels of land and sea, and it may well be that this edge represents very closely the original eastern shore-line as deposited by the glacier. But this was many thousands of years ago.

It is probable that in a comparatively short time after the melting ice-cap left the outermost sandbank exposed to the unrestrained attack of the tides and waves of the North Atlantic, the outer beach had straightened out into something resembling the pattern of today, although lying somewhat farther east and lacking the Provincetown and Monomoy extensions. Every tide, every rolling breaker, even every gust of wind, shifted it a little, just as it does today. What was chewed off in one place was spewed up in another. But the frontier of walking sands was always there, taking the brunt of the sea, with always a new replacement to meet the new breaker, as changeable, yet as eternal, as the ocean which it held in check.

For thousands of years this outer barrier has made an orderly retreat. It has fallen slowly back like an obstinate rear-guard. It persistently holds its protecting riband outside and back of everything else—harbor, headland, or what-not. When finally forced inland, the ocean makes short work of any upland left exposed through its seaward side, and soon the outer beach is back to its normal appearance again.[1] Thus, through the centuries, the Back Side of Cape Cod presents much the same aspect to the mariner coasting its shores. If Leif Ericson and his hardy Norse shipmates sighted it from their long ship a thousand years ago, it undoubtedly struck their vision much as it did the Pilgrims from the deck of the *Mayflower* in 1620, and as it still looks to the shoals fisherman setting his trawl offshore along the 'Edge' today.

The idea that a steady rate of retrogression from year to year is taking place along the whole length of the Back Side is erroneous. At Highland Light in Truro, and alongshore north and south of it for a few miles, this is more or less true, although even here there are periods when no appreciable recession occurs. But north of it, opposite High Head, an outer protective beach with a creek and marshland between it and the mainland was built up long before the day of the Pilgrims,[2] and is there today. South of Eastham we find the same formation outside the harbors of Nauset and Pleasant Bay. Except for the cutting-away of the old point outside of Nauset Harbor, there seems to have been very little recession in the shore-line here for centuries.

At Chatham Light, on James's Head, owing to the peculiar local conditions to which it is exposed, the currents of the shifting harbor mouth eat

away the beach in front of it occasionally, and take a bite out of the mainland itself. This is what happened when the old lighthouses tumbled down
the bank years ago. While this is of local importance, spread over miles of
coast and a century of history, it is of small moment. It illustrates the falla-
cy of basing calculations as to recession of the general coast-line on records
of some particular locality for a short period of time.

As a matter of fact, except for the straightening-out of the Back Side
through the washing-away of outjutting points from time to time, and the
filling-in of the harbors and bends with the débris, neither the history of
modern surveys nor a comparison with ancient landmarks and records shows
that any far-fetched and radical changes in the coast-line have taken place
since the period of 1620.

With this truth in mind we can go ahead much more intelligently in following the ancient mariners along the shore to see what they found.

The contemporary source material giving definite information concerning the Back Side around 1620 is very limited. Besides the account given in
Mourt's Relation and the Bradford history of the *Mayflower*'s experience on
approaching the land, which I will take up in its proper place, there are the
accounts of Captain Bartholomew Gosnold's voyage in 1602 as described by
Archer and Brereton who accompanied him; Sieur de Champlain's voyages
of 1605 and 1606 with the accompanying maps of these and his other
explorations; the voyage of Captain John Smith to New England in 1614
and the map he made at that time without the later additions; Dermer's letters describing his 1619 passage around the Cape; Winslow's 'Good News
from New England' in which he describes Governor Bradford's attempt to
pass to the southward of the Cape in 1622; Bradford's own account of the
same attempt, and his trip in 1626 to the succor of the ill-fated *Sparrowhawk*
in old Monomoyick Bay.

There is much interesting collateral material to be found in various other
accounts, but not giving anything of specific value for my purpose.
Weymouth, on the fourteenth of May, 1605, ran afoul of the shoals off
Nantucket in latitude 41° 20′ north, sighted the white banks of Sankaty, got
scared off, and did not make the land again until he raised the coast of
Maine;[3] Hudson landed in latitude 41° 45′ north, the third of August,
1609,[4] which, if his reckoning was good, was at old Monomoyick Bay, now
Pleasant Bay. He then continued on south, outside the Shoals and
Nantucket. Argall, on the twentieth of August, 1611, sighted the Cape in
latitude 41° 44′ north,[5] and then continued on south, probably following
Hudson's route; the same year Harlow sailed all around the Cape and as far
south as the Vineyard, undoubtedly negotiating the Shoals, but leaving
nothing by way of description;[6] 1614 found Admiral Blok in the Onrust

exploring the coast from New York to Boston,[7] which resulted in the Dutch map embodying much of what the French and English had already learned, as well as his own discoveries; and there were others.

There are also a host of maps dating from 1500 to 1700, each showing the Cape in some form or other, but, with the exception of those made as the result of the voyages of Champlain, few have any value whatever as guides to the conditions of the Back Side at the time the *Mayflower* arrived.[8] Captain Smith summed them up succinctly when he said they were not worth as much as so much waste paper. With the exception of the French charts, which he had probably never seen, this was too true. It held good for the next hundred years so far as detailed information concerning the Back Side of Cape Cod went.

For the contemporary picture I have confined myself to the sources before mentioned, namely: Gosnold, Champlain, Smith, Dermer, Winslow, and Bradford, purposely leaving out for the present what the *Mayflower* party found in 1620 so that I may prove from other sources what the Back Side was like at the period she came on to it.

From the details given in Archer's account of Gosnold's voyage,[9] which in a general way is substantiated by Brereton's account of the same voyage,[10] we learn that about twelve leagues southerly from the point near which they had anchored and named Cape Cod, they arrived at a point of land with some outlying bars. Twelve leagues, or thirty-six miles, from their anchorage at Long Point, Provincetown, would bring them just about to Nauset Harbor. From the text it is plainly evident that it was neither a very prominent point of land they had arrived at, nor were the bars very difficult to sail around. Otherwise they would not have passed around it and anchored in under the shore south of it in eight fathoms of water before night, as they say they did, without even sending a boat ahead to sound it out. Even the name given to the bars, Tucker's Terror, appears to have been applied more in a humorous than in a serious vein, as if the terror with which Master's Mate Tucker was inspired was not participated in by the other officers. They named the point of land inside the bars Point Care. This was on the sixteenth of May, 1602. Had they been as bold and inquisitive explorers as Champlain, or had their ship been smaller and of lighter draught so they could have stood in nearer, they would have found that there was a harbor inside Tucker's Terror, and that Point Care marked its entrance and outer barrier.

Three years later, on the nineteenth of July, 1605, the French under Sieur de Monts, accompanied by Samuel de Champlain,[11] anchored near the same bars, sent in a boat to the sandy point, and discovered the bay inside. The next day they went in with their ship, passing the bar with breakers all around them. They remained at anchor inside until the twenty-fifth, when they nearly lost their ship on the bar in going out. They named the place 'Malle-barre,' 'Bad bar,' not because it was a bad bar to sail *around,* but because it was bad to *cross* on entering and leaving harbor, as it is today.

Sailing northeasterly [12] eighteen miles, on their homeward passage to the St. Croix River, they came opposite what they had previously named Cape Blanc when running down to Malle-barre. This is about the correct distance from Nauset to the Head of Cape Cod, the place from which they would logically shape their course for the Eastern Shore. From here they took a departure to sight Cape Ann and make the Maine coast.

Fortunately, Champlain left a remarkably fine map of this harbor as it then was,[13] showing the entrance about midway of the outer beach, with their ship anchored inside. The name `Deep Water Point' still clings to the relative spot where his ship lay at anchor, although both the deep water and the point have long since shifted to other locations.

To the north of the entrance a low, sandy beach tailed down from the Eastham shore. Here, between the 20th and 25th of July, 1605, one of Champlain's companions, a man of St. Malo, was killed in a scrimmage with the Indians. The French buried him among the beach knolls directly north of the harbor's mouth. This, I believe, is the first authentic record of the death and burial of a white man on our shores. South of the channel was a point of land much higher and broader, covered 'with low shrubs and many vines.' The fact that it is shown on the map as supporting a substantial growth of trees proves to any one familiar with the land formation along the Back Side that this point was either the remains of a detached part of the mainland or an old island, even though it was at that time connected to the mainland of East Orleans south of it by a narrow neck of sand. Its location is identical with the bushy, rocky islet which has come down to us in history as the famous Ile of Nausit,[14] known to our fathers under the intriguing appellation of 'Slut's Bush,'[15] from the little swamp of vines and shrubs in its midst.

When Champlain returned to Malle-barre the following year, on the second of October, 1606, Sieur de Poutrincourt landed on this point while they were delayed by head winds, to view the harbor, leaving the ship outside the bar. They later passed on to the southward without any difficulty when the wind became favorable.[16] Neither on his map of Malle-barre, nor in his description of this visit, does Champlain mention any appreciable change from what he found the year before. During the winter of 1606-07, following his voyage of 1605 to Nauset and that of 1606 down by Nauset and in around Monomoy Point, he made a general map of the whole coast, including the Back Side of the Cape,[17] but neither on this nor on any of his later maps is there the slightest indication of any shoals of a dangerous nature stretching offshore any great distance from Nauset.[18] Champlain was a keen observer, and it is certain he would have somewhere noted such a danger had one existed at that period.

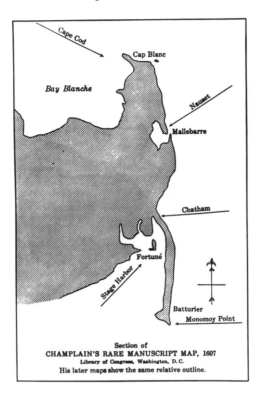

Section of
CHAMPLAIN'S RARE MANUSCRIPT MAP, 1607
Library of Congress, Washington, D. C.
His later maps show the same relative outline.

Figure 4. Section of Champlain's Map of Cape Cod, 1607.

Therefore, there is no reason to suppose, when Gosnold doubled this place, which he named Point Care, in 1602, that it, nor the bars outside of it, lay very differently from their position three years later, when Champlain mapped and described it so painstakingly. It is obvious that the Point Care of Gosnold was the shrubby, vine-covered point described by Champlain, but it is exceedingly doubtful that in three years' time it had receded more than a few rods at the most unless under extremely extraordinary circumstances.

Captain John Smith mentions the same place when he notes what the Indians told him about the shoals lying south and southwest of Cape Cod.[19] He himself went only so far south by the Cape on his 1614 voyage as he could carry thirty 'fadom water aboard the shore,' which would not have taken him much, if any, south of Peaked Hill, at the Head of the Cape. Captain Smith, like most of the honest-to-God explorers, was pretty careful not to vouch for anything he did not see with his own eyes, and the Ile of Nausit was one of them. He says he took the Indians' word for it that the 'shoales beginne from the main at Pawmet, to the Ile of Nausit, and so extends beyond their knowledge into the sea.'

This description is as true today as it was then, and identifies the Point Care of Gosnold, the Malle-barre of Champlain, and the Ile of Nausit which the Indians told Smith about, as one and the same place, then as now the beginning of that stretch of harbor bars stringing along outside of Nauset, tailing down by the entrance to old Monomoyick Bay—now known as Pleasant Bay—and culminating south of Chatham Bars in the Shoals of Pollack Rip.[20]

Bradford corroborates this in his comments on the names which certain places on the Cape had received prior to his arrival. He says that 'Capten Gosnole and his company' called the 'pointe which first shewed those dangerous shoulds unto them' 'Point Care' and 'Tuckers Terrour, but the French and Dutch to this day call it Malle Barre.'[21] It is plain from the text that Bradford referred to it as the place where Gosnold first encountered dangerous shoals while skirting along the coast close in, and not in any sense whatever as the spot where the *Mayflower* turned back, as has been suggested by various writers.[22]

The subsequent disintegration of old Point Care is easily traceable. It came to be known as Slut's Bush as early as 1659 at least,[23] and perhaps much earlier.[24] At a town meeting held July 6, 1743, making a division of the common land in the south part of Eastham—now Orleans—it is located as a 'place on Pocha beach called Slut's bush on the southerly side of the Harbor called Stage Harbor' and east from 'the highland of the Stage.'[25] Stage Harbor was an early name of Nauset Harbor, and the highlands of the Stage are still a landmark. Placing Slut's Bush east from it puts it exactly on a line with the shrubby point of land which Champlain shows as being south of the harbor entrance one hundred and thirty-eight years before.

In an unrecorded deed, dated April 1, 1790, mention is made of 'stage mill against Slush-Bush.'[26] Up to about 1800 it appears that the Slut's Bush in the middle of the point or island, from which it took its name, was still intact, a rocky huckleberry swamp that the sea had not as yet eaten into.

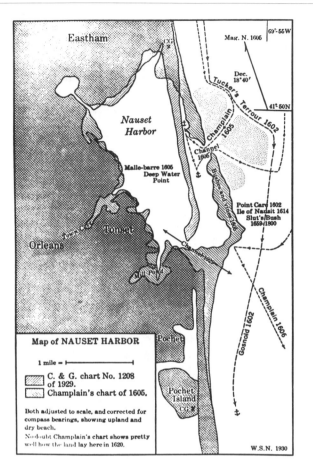

Figure 5. Champlain's Map of Nauset Harbor in 1605

By 1815, only the very western edge of the swamp remained, and south of it, inside the neck of beach connecting it with the mainland, was a ten-acre salt marsh belonging to the Doanes.[27] By 1833, point, island, and swamp had disappeared, a new channel had opened through the neck south of it, and the north beach had made down across the ancient entrance of Malle-barre, almost as far as it is today,[28] and by 1863, a deep channel was running out to sea right where the old Doane meadows lay a hundred years before.[29]

Even to this day, to my own personal knowledge, relics of the old island come to light after a heavy easterly—rocks, old roots and stumps, great hunks of salt marsh. On the latest charts of the Coast and Geodetic Survey its site is marked by the telltale shoal bending a mile offshore into the deeper water on either side,[30] and the fisherman knows it well.

In 1863, John Doane testified that the beach outside the harbor had moved inland about its own width, or about one quarter of a mile, within his memory. He was then seventy years old.[31] What was left of his meadow was being buried by it, and he no doubt observed it pretty closely. For the sixty years after 1800, this was probably very nearly true, but it is fair to assume that previous to that time, while the tough old remnant of Slut's Bush still withstood the brunt of the sea, the recession was not any faster than under like conditions elsewhere. My personal observations of the rate at which old headlands recede while still protected by outlying bars lead me to think that a rate of over twelve feet a year from 1620 to 1800 would be excessive, or less than half a mile for the whole period. This, added to the possible quarter of a mile from 1800 to 1860, would give not over three quarters of a mile recession up to that time, and a comparison of the recent surveys with those of 1860 shows that there has been very little since. Superimposing Champlain's map of 1605, corrected to scale and for magnetic declination, on the chart of 1929 shows a close agreement with this calculation, and proves without a shadow of a doubt that he gives a very accurate picture of the locality at that period.

With the debatable region around Nauset Harbor eliminated as a possible dangerous hazard to a southward passage of the *Mayflower*, or any other ship of that period, we can proceed on down the shore toward Chatham with the ancient mariners.

After Gosnold rounded Point Care, at Nauset, on the sixteenth of May, 1602, he stood close in under the land south of it and anchored for the night in eight fathoms of water, on good holding ground. Here he lay at anchor during the seventeenth because of head winds and the many breakers near him. While lying here he observed two inlets through the beach, and the Indians came off in their canoes to trade.[32]

Without much question this anchorage was the hard bottom in the deep water southeast of Pochet Coast Guard Station, just north of the harbor bars then lying outside of the old entrance to Pleasant Bay. Weather-bound shoals fishermen still seek an anchorage here under the weather shore in stiff nor'westers. Inside the beach lay the almost landlocked stretch of waters variously designated in the early records as Sutcliffe's Inlets, Monomoyick Bay, Potnomocut Harbor, and Middle Harbor.[33] The inlets he mentions were the crooked, sand-choked channels leading into it.

In 1619, Dermer entered 'Manamock (the southern part of Cape Cod, now called Sutcliffe's Inlets),' where he was taken prisoner by the Indians and narrowly escaped with his life.[34] Bradford put back into 'Manamoyack

Bay' in the *Swan*, about the 'latter end of September,' 1622, sounding in through a 'narrow and crooked' channel, after trying to 'get aboute ye should of Cap-Cod' without success with Squanto as a guide. In this Bay Squanto sickened and died of an Indian fever, and his remains lie somewhere around its beautiful shores. There seemed to be another inlet into the Bay, but because of bad weather, Bradford was unable to locate it.[35]

In the fall of 1626, Bradford came again to this same place to the succor of the ill-fated *Sparrowhawk* and her company, which 'came so neare ye shoulds of Cap-Cod or else ran stumbling over them in ye night,' and was stranded in 'a small blind harbore, that lyes about ye midle of Manamoyake Bay, to ye southward of Cap-Cod.'[36] The finding of the hulk of the *Sparrowhawk* in 1782 where she was wrecked in 1626, and the subsequent salvaging of it in 1865, while an interesting incident in the history of old Monomoyick Bay, has been well covered in the admirable little booklet published by Alfred Mudge and Son, Boston, 1865,[37] but because her resting-place identifies the location of the 'small blind harbore' of 1626, and thereby all other contemporary references both to the Bay and its entrance, I feel that an additional word is not amiss.

The *Sparrowhawk* went aground and was buried in the sands at a place which later grew up to meadow and became known as the 'Old Ship Lot,' or lot Number 2, in the Potonomocut Propriety. When the Propriety was laid out, before 1750, it was the second lot north of the entrance to the Harbor.[38] My father, who was about thirty years old when she was exhumed the last time, owned salt meadow lying near this spot and has often pointed it out to me. It was about a mile south of Pochet Island and a little more than that north of the Orleans-Chatham boundary on the beach, very near what is known today as the Bass Hole. It lies about due east from the middle of the Pleasant Bay of today, the ancient Monomoyick Bay of the days of the *Mayflower,* and the Bass Hole without doubt represents the ancient channel. Outside the beach is a fishing ground known to this day as the 'Old Ship Ground,' but there are few men who fish there that know why it is thus called.

From here let us proceed on with Gosnold. On the eighteenth of May, 1602, while still at anchor off Monomoyick Bay, he sent a boat to sound around a shoal which lay off a point of land ahead, which he named Gilbert's Point. Up until this time he had not run afoul of shoal water serious enough to cause him to send out a boat to sound it out. The latitude of Gilbert's Point he found to be 41° 40' north, and its estimated distance from Point Care, or Nauset, about twelve miles.[39] Both its distance from Nauset and its latitude coincide exactly with that 'narrow tongue of land' stretching out from North Chatham, and so carefully delineated on the map of Port Fortune made by Champlain four years later, and leaves no question whatever as to the location of Gosnold's Gilbert's Point.[40]

On the second of October, 1606, Champlain, on his second voyage to the Cape, after touching at Nauset, worked south along the coast against a head wind a distance which he estimated as eighteen miles, and then anchored.[41] This could not have been south of Chatham, in spite of the estimated distance, or he would not have been visited by the Indians in their canoes, nor observed their fires on the shore. Beating down back of the Cape in the little craft he was in, against a head wind, is sufficient reason for overestimating his distance. The Indians told him that lower down would be found a harbor for his ship. There is little question that this stopping-place was very near the Gilbert's Point of Gosnold, off the present town of Chatham. His map[42] of this locality, which I have mentioned, was so accurate that it is not at all difficult to reconstruct the shore-line of 1606 from known landmarks still remaining.

As far south as Chatham no voyager records any body of shoals lying offshore sufficiently far to be a menace to the navigation of a southbound ship. Gosnold and Champlain, in 1602, 1605, and 1606, hugging close along the shore, found the harbor bars of Nauset and old Monomoyick Bay relatively as they are today.[43] Hudson, and most of the other coasters, after getting down into about the latitude of Chatham, hauled off and gave the coast a wide berth. Bradford, in 1622, mentions nothing until he is far enough south to head back to Monomoyick Bay. In fact, there is nothing to show that the men who were there during this period found anything to bother them much until they passed to the southward of Chatham. From this point on, they are all equally emphatic as to the extremely dangerous nature of the outlying shoals.

Gosnold, on the nineteenth of May, 1602, left his anchorage north of Gilbert's Point—Chatham—rounded it, and anchored again about three or four miles south of it.[44] Three or four miles south of Chatham would bring him about to what is known today as Stewart's Bend. This has been an anchoring ground from very early times. Before 1713, William Eldredge built a house there and opened a tavern for sailors, which about 1725 became the property of Joseph Stewart, probably the former owner of the land. From him the locality took the name of Stewart's Knoll, and the anchorage east of it became known as Stewart's Bend.[45] In 1833, it is described as a place 'on the east side of Cape Malebar[46] or the sandy point of Chatham,' where ships could ride in three or four fathoms, sheltered from winds from north to southwest, lying about three miles south of the mainland.[47] In 1893, it is given as an anchorage having two and a half to five fathoms of water.[48] It is there today, designated on the late charts of the Coast and Geodetic Survey as Old Harbor, or Schooner Bar,[49] but the fishermen still call it Stewart's Bend. This represents the same anchorage which Gosnold found in 1602.

Here Gosnold hung on until the twenty-first, when he got under way, stood off into ten fathoms of water, on an east-by-south course, shoaled it to six fathoms near the shore, and finally rounded the point which they had taken to be an island, being obliged to give it a three-mile berth in order to find three fathoms of water in through the shoals. He named the point Shoal Hope, a name they had given to the Cape at Provincetown previously, but changed when they found no passage west of it. After passing in over the Shoals at Shoal Hope, he continued on, to winter at the Elizabeth Islands.[50]

Gosnold's east-by-south course, from his anchorage three or four miles south of Chatham in Stewart's Bend, would carry him well clear of the northeast point of Bearse's Shoal as it lies today, and into ten fathoms of water. Continuing on about three miles along the outer edge of what is now the Broken Part of Pollack Rip would bring him to the old channel south of it known as the Southeast Slue.[51] Here he would get into six fathoms of water, or even three, as he says, or less, unless he was lucky enough to keep in the very best of it. From his description and the bearings given, it is fair to assume that he found his Shoal Hope lying very near what is now the northeast end of Bearse's Shoal. With this in mind, let us come down to Champlain's experience four years later in the same place.

Champlain left his anchorage off Chatham, somewhere very near Gilbert's Point, on the third of October, 1606, and sailing a distance estimated at less than fifteen miles, he found himself getting into three and four fathoms of water three miles and more from a point which ran out seaward to the south-southeast from Chatham a distance of nearly nine miles. The water soon shoaled to one and a half and two fathoms with breakers all around, but the wind being from the north he could not turn back and so was forced to let his ship go wherever he could find water enough to float her, sometimes getting into as little as four and a half feet, with his ship drawing four. At last, by dint of good luck, he got around the sandy point,[52] which he called Cape Batturier, and a 'very dangerous place.'[53]

Champlain locates his Cape Batturier about nine miles south-southeast from Chatham, and the 'very dangerous place' where he pounded in over the Shoals as three miles and more beyond it. The distance and bearing from Chatham which he gives fixes his Cape Batturier approximately at the northeast extremity of Bearse's Shoal, and his course intersects that of Gosnold just to the northeast of it in about ten fathoms of water, from which point they both continued on three or four miles before they found an opening through the Shoals.

Here we have two clear and lucid descriptions of the southern extremity of Cape Cod and the beginning of the Shoals of Pollack Rip, by two keen observers. Gosnold steered east by south in 1602 from his anchorage in Stewart's Bend, rounded a point which he had supposed to be an island, called it Shoal Hope—as indeed it was—passed it at a distance of three miles off in three fathoms of water, and continued on in over the Shoals. Champlain, leaving his anchorage off Chatham in 1606, passed a sandy point lying about nine miles south-southeast, and pounded in over the Shoals, three miles or more beyond it, naming it Cape Batturier. Taking each description at its face value and correcting the courses to agree approximately with the variation of their compasses as of that period,[54] it is surprising how closely they agree in results. Their courses and distances illustrate this better than any words of mine, and leave little doubt that the Shoal Hope of Gosnold, the Cape Batturier of Champlain, and the northeast end of Bearse's Shoal today, are in the same relative position. With this fact demonstrated, let us see if there is any reason for it in the history of Bearse's Shoal.

In the first place, all of the earliest maps which are worth considering at all, including the rare manuscript map of 1606-07 by Champlain,[55] clearly show that the representative of what we know as Monomoy Point, or Island, today, stretched in a generally southerly direction from the mainland at Chatham from the very earliest times, relatively as it is shown on the very latest chart of the Coast and Geodetic Survey. Bearse's Shoal and the adjacent Broken Part of Pollack Rip hook out easterly from the southern extremity of Monomoy Point into the same position occupied by Shoal Hope in 1602 and Cape Batturier in 1606; that is, about nine miles southeasterly from Chatham and easterly from Stewart's Bend.

A little over a hundred years later, we find Captain Cyprian Southack showing the same place as Wreck Point, illustrated on his charts as located just about on the site of the northeast part of Bearse's Shoal, and hooking out easterly in a more or less triangular point from what he designates as Webb's Island.[56] He places Webb's Island almost exactly on what the Coast and Geodetic Survey today name as Monomoy Island. This Webb's Island is known to history and tradition as lying off about nine miles southeasterly from Stage Harbor, Chatham, where the Nantucketers used to come to cut firewood and ferry it home.[57] That it lay in close proximity to the present Monomoy Point is evidenced by the washing-up on the east side, as late as 1850, of old stumps still bearing the axe-marks of the early Nantucketers.[58]

Southack's charts show 'Seal Islands, Sunken,' lying south of Wreck Point and Webb's Island. In 1833, Webb's or Monomoy Island was separated from the mainland by a shallow channel half a mile wide at high water,[59] and Southack's map indicates that in his day the narrow neck of sand lying off Chatham, and called by Gosnold Gilbert's Point, had, in the last hundred years, been cut through at its northern end, and had worked inshore so that it nearly lapped on to Webb's Island, probably very near where the shallow channel was in 1833.

In 1800, the 'American Coast Pilot' gives an up-to-date chart showing Bearse's Shoal as a dry bar with two fathoms of water on its outer end.[60] This depth compares with the sixteen feet found there today. In 1832, parts of it were still entirely dry, as well as the rips to the southeast of it, and in 1843, these rips had gradually flattened down and extended eastward showing three feet of water in their shoalest parts. By 1852, this had deepened to six feet, and in 1882, to eight feet in the same places. But as late as 1893, Bearse's Shoal itself was nearly dry at low water,[61] and today there are places on it showing as little as five feet at mean low tide, as many a sailor knows to his sorrow. The latest reports from the Coast and Geodetic Survey show that the water here is very gradually growing deeper, and the eastern edge of the Broken Part of Pollack Rip is very slowly working to the eastward, if anything.[62] I have talked with old fishermen who still call this section the 'Dry Part of Pollack Rip.' All the known facts indicate that at the period when the *Mayflower* came onto the coast, Bearse's Shoal was dry land, a low, sandy point, which even today is barely covered at low water.

At present the dredged channel runs just south of Bearse's Shoal, between it and Pollack Rip. Within my memory it ran south of Pollack Rip, between it and the Broken Part, and in 1832, it was south of all three, opening out to sea through what was known as the Southeast Slue.[63] It is most significant that Southack's maps show the 'Channel Way' in exactly this same position about 1720, some three or four miles south of where he locates Wreck Point, with the soundings approximating very closely those found there to this day. This old 'Way' corresponds in almost every detail with the descriptions given by Champlain and Gosnold of the way they found in over the Shoals. In 1833, Blunt gives the following sailing directions from Chatham south and in over the Shoals: 'From Chatham Lights steer S.S.E. 3½ leagues, when you will pass Pollack Rip in 3 or 4 fathoms of water, then W. ½ S. 5 miles into Butler's Hole.' He adds that Chatham Lights bear N.N.W. from the entrance to the Shoals.[64] A comparison with Champlain will show almost the same words for the same passage in 1606, and it is as good today as it was then.

I could go on indefinitely piling up the evidence that Bearse's Shoal represents today the Shoal Hope of Gosnold, the Cape Batturier of Champlain, the Wreck Point of Southack; and that the Broken Part of Pollack Rip represents the shoal bars they found stretching off beyond it for three or four miles, with the 'Channel Way' over the Shoals entering in south of it. If we could, by a magic touch, raise the level of these old shoals a few feet, we should see very nearly what *they* saw. That they took their ships through this treacherous labyrinth at all is the highest kind of testimonial to their cool courage and ability.

We are too prone to approach the Back Side of the Cape with the bias that it is changing swiftly and radically. We are too disposed to throw over the entries in the logs of the ancient navigators because they do not seem to fit our preconceived ideas of what they should be. As a matter of fact, the changes on the Back Side have been orderly and relatively slow as a general thing, and closely adhering to well-recognized laws and causes easily traced backward by an observing son of the sands. The old mariners knew their sailors' book much better than the learned men who take it upon themselves to make corrections. Almost invariably, if one will painstakingly adjust their descriptions to the compass conditions, the wind, weather and tides as they found them, and reconstruct the shore-line to correspond to their day, he will find that they were as near right as was humanly possible under the handicaps with which they were working.

To sum up: It appears that north of Nauset Harbor, to High Head in Truro, the general shore-line may have lain offshore a little from what it does today, not over a third of a mile at most. Outside Nauset Harbor, the original Malle-barre of the Frenchmen, lay the Point Care of Gosnold, later known as the 'Ile of Nausit,' or 'Slut's Bush.' It may possibly have jutted out a third of a mile beyond the general shore-line, with the usual harbor bars making out a short distance farther, perhaps another quarter of a mile, much as they do today.

South of Nauset, as long as the remnant of Point Care remained to deflect the southern drift inward around it, the result would be an inward curve of the beach for some miles, and this is what Champlain's map of 1606-07, and Gosnold's description in 1602 indicate. The bold bluffs and well-worn eastern headlands of the islands, now lying snugly protected in Pleasant Bay behind the outlying beaches, also point to more than the sluggish wash of landlocked waters.[65] About a mile south of Pochet Island was the inlet into old Monomoyick Bay where the *Sparrowhawk* was wrecked, and farther on toward Chatham still another, probably just north of where the old Harbor Coast Guard Station is today. Just beyond this, making out boldly from North Chatham in an easterly direction toward the present

Coast Guard Station, was a sandy neck of beach, forming Gilbert's Point at a place very near where it would intersect with the present outer beach near the Station, and then turning abruptly south and following relatively the present beach and harbor bars, forming an arm of the sea half a mile wide east of Chatham and enclosing the old island of Cotchpinecote, or Ram Island, in its northern end. The site of this island and the beach north of it is plainly identified today by Ram Island Flat and the Mussel Beds north of it.[66]

Still farther south, occupying approximately the position shown on the present-day charts as Monomoy Island, was Webb's Island, with probably a stretch of tidal flats and sandy bars between it and Gilbert's Point north of it. Hooking out easterly from its southern end was the sandy point now marked by Bearse's Shoal, known at various periods as Shoal Hope, Cape Batturier, Vlaecke Hoecke, Wreck Point, and other names now gone into the discard. Beyond this were the dreaded 'shoulds of Cap-Cod,' sometimes called the Great Riff of Malabar, and a 'very dangerous place.'

Nowhere in the records or charts of the men who actually became acquainted with the Back Side at this early period do we find one iota of evidence to indicate that anywhere north of what we know today as Bearse's Shoal did they encounter anything anywhere, other than the usual outlying harbor bars. To a careful and skilful navigator, as we are certain Captain Jones was, these were no more than the ordinary perils of a strange coast. We may, therefore, count out from the reckoning of the *Mayflower* all other obstacles to a southward passage until she arrives at the Shoals of Pollack Rip.

In short, the man who stood on the deck of the *Mayflower* three hundred years ago, and fixed the landmarks of the Back Side of Cape Cod in his mind, would have little difficulty in recognizing them today. There would be the Highland of Truro, with its seamed and weatherbeaten face of clay, defying the challenge of the sea. There would be the low, wooded shores of Eastham, rising from their sandy beaches and stretching back into the distant tableland. Point Care and Ile Nausit would be gone, but the 'bad bars' of Nauset Harbor would still break white, and other islands would show their heads behind the outer beach. Gilbert's Point would be marked by the Harbor Bars of Chatham, with the Great Hill still in place behind them. While the old Cape Batturier, or Shoal Hope, would no longer lift its sandy point above the waves, its site on Bearse's Shoal would still be as much a barrier as ever its low-lying dunes were; and our captain would find the dangerous shoals and roaring breakers, which turned him back from Virginia, just about where he left them at sunset on the night of the ninth of November, 1620.

I have gone into the probable configuration of the coast-line of 1620, or thereabouts, quite at length, not only because it is the crucial point in the whole question of the *Mayflower*'s several positions for the three days she spent off back of the Cape, but because there has always been a great deal of controversy over where the shoals lay which turned her back on the ninth.

While she was running south down the Back Side, she certainly was not hugging the beach looking for possible harbors, and running afoul of the inevitable outlying harbor-bars, as Gosnold and Champlain had done. She was a deeply laden ship, giving the shore a reasonable berth, and to all intents and purposes bound south around the Cape, until she suddenly ran into something serious enough to turn her back on her course. Until she got well down by Chatham, there was nothing to interfere with her southward passage, any more than there is today for a ship sailing a similar course. 'The shoulds of Cap-Cod' are still 'The Shoals,' and will be for some centuries to come, I presume. There are no others worthy the name for a hundred miles to the north, and I hope I have demonstrated sufficiently that there were not three centuries ago.

The tidal currents affect very materially the passage of any sailing ship— or any other ship, for that matter—up and down the Back Side of Cape Cod. Hence it is absolutely necessary to know them well and reckon with them closely in determining the *Mayflower*'s position at any time after she came in sight of land.

A general explanation of the eccentricities peculiar to the tides in this particular locality may help the reader to a clearer understanding of why certain conclusions seem inevitable, when I later take up each day's work hour by hour.

Broadly speaking, the great flood tide, following on the heels of the moon from east to west across the Atlantic, strikes the sharp elbow of the Cape and splits locally into two distinct currents almost opposite Nauset Light.[67] One current of flood turns sharply north and sweeps up along the shores of Wellfleet and Truro, and finally races in around Race Point at Provincetown to make high tide in Cape Cod Bay. The time of high water at the Head of the Cape and the turn of the tide coincide very closely with that at Nauset.

The other current of flood turns as sharply south from Nauset and flows down close in by Orleans and Chatham toward the Shoals. But here, instead of running its logical six-hour course and turning north again, it joins the ebb or westerly current setting in over the Shoals into the Sound,[68] where the time of high water is materially earlier than at Nauset. The result is that the turn of the tide on the Shoals is governed by that inside the Shoals rather than that to the north of it.

The difference in time at the entrance to the Shoals is approximately two hours and a half, under normal conditions,[69] thus causing the southern tide to slack and turn at the Shoals about that much later than at Nauset, and *vice versa* for the next tide, or ebb. Owing to this, a ship leaving Nauset at the right time of tide may hold either a fair or a head tide for eight or nine hours if she takes that time to run to the Shoals.

This may sound a bit complicated to the landsman, and it is only fair to state that it is to any but the most experienced and able navigators, but any one navigating a square-rigged ship along this coast must of necessity know these tides minutely, or he will not get far. It is, if anything, more necessary than an understanding of the local magnetic declination of the compass-needle.

Notes

1. 'The relative order of sandbanks and beaches remains about the same, however the system as a whole may change its location.' *Massachusetts Harbor Commissioners Report,* 1873, p. 99, by Prof. Mitchell.
2. East Harbor Creek. See Mourt, 17. Bradford, 98.
3. *Massachusetts Historical Society Collections,* 3d Series, 8:131.
4. Jouet's *Account of Hudson's Voyage,* New York Historical Society Collections, 1:121. [Robert Juet. Page 18 in printing listed in bibliography. August 1: 41° 45′; August 2: 41° 56′; August 3: not noted but identified by Juet's editor as "the north shore of Cape Cod"; August 4: 41° 45′ but noted by Juet's editor as "This is quite likely Cape Cod, although there is considerable disagreement." They went on land on both 3 and 4 August.]
5. *Purchas' Pilgrims,* part 4, 1761.
6. Smith's *History of Chatham,* 1:65. [Smith was originally printed in four parts. Page 25 as in bibliography.]
7. *Memorial History of Boston,* 1:57.
8. See Verrazano's, Ribero's, Mercator's, Berteli's, Ortelius's, DeLaet's, Wood's, Seller's, Hubbard's, etc.
9. *Massachusetts Historical Society Collections,* 3d Series, 8:74.
10. *Ibid.,* 8:86, 87.
11. *Voyages of Sieur de Champlain,* Prince Society Edition, 2:80, 81. [79-81]
12. The Prince Society translation says they made a north*east* course for six leagues which brought them off Cape Blanc (Cape Cod), and then continued this course until they were opposite Island Cape (Cape Ann). A footnote says this course should have been north*west.* Apparently the author of the note takes no account of the local declination of the magnetic needle. Champlain himself says it was 18° 40′ west at Nauset. This would give a compass course to pass Cape Ann, just in sight, of approximately N. by E. He also says that the declination near the mouth

of the Kennebec, where he was heading, was 19° 12′, even more than it was at Nauset. He would allow a little easterly for this. He undoubtedly left Nauset on the flood tide. A point allowance easterly for the west tide sweeping him in by the head of Cape Cod would not be at all improbable, and would make good a course of N.N.E. North*west* by his compass would have piled him up on the beach in less than half an hour. [90, text and note 174]

13. *Voyages of Sieur de Champlain*, 2:81. [Map faces 82; see note 167 on 81 and Champlain's explanation of the map on 82.]
14. Captain Smith's *Description of New England*, Veazie, 1865, p. 45.
15. *The* Mayflower *Descendant*, 22:167, 168; Stanley W. Smith Collection; Amos Otis Papers. [Slush-Bush]
16. *Voyages of Sieur de Champlain*, 2:118, 119, Map 2:81. [117; map faces 82.]
17. See map, Library of Congress, copy on p. 4, vol. III, *France and New England*, State Street Trust Company Publications.
18. See 1612 map, *France and New England*, 3:1 [*xviii*, facing p. 1]; 1632 map, *ibid.*, 3:23 [p. 22]; Lescarbot's map, 1609, Winsor's *Narrative and Critical History of America.*
19. Smith, *Description of New England*, 45.
20. See Coast and Geodetic Survey charts 1208 and 1209.
21. Bradford, 94. ['Capten Gosnole & his company' called the 'pointe which first shewed those dangerous shoulds unto them' 'Pointe Care,' & 'Tuckers Terrour; but ye French & Dutch to this day call it Malabarr.']
22. The theory of Mr. Amos Otis, supported by Professor Agassiz, and having the quasi-endorsement of Mr. Henry M. Dexter, that Point Care lay some three miles offshore near Briar's Ledge, has no support by actual historical facts. While all they suggest, and more, may have been true in prehistoric times, the contemporary records prove it was not so anywhere near the period of 1620.
23. W. C. Smith's *History of Chatham*, 1:26.
24. It has been suggested to me that this name may have been a corruption of a Dutch name applied to the island because of the shrubby growth there.
25. Stanley W. Smith Collections.
26. *The* Mayflower *Descendant*, 22:167, 168.
27. Otis, *New England Historical and Genealogical Register*, 18:37-44. [43]
28. Blunt's *American Coast Pilot*, 187, 188.
29. See note 27, above, for reference. [43]
30. Coast and Geodetic Survey chart 1208.
31. See note 27, above, for reference. [43]
32. Archer, *Massachusetts Historical Society Collections*, 3d Series, 8:74, 75.
33. Besides Dermer, Bradford, and others, see Eastham and Harwich town and propriety records, and Plymouth Records for names.
34. Dermer's Letter, Purchas, *New York Historical Society Collections*, 2d Series; Bradford, 118. [Manamoiak (a place not farr from hence, now well knowne)]
35. Bradford, 155; Winslow's *Relation*; Young's *Chronicles*, 300.

36. Bradford, 261, 262. [Cap-Codd]
37. Stanley W. Smith Collections.
38. Otis, *New England Historical and Genealogical Register*, 18:37. [41]
39. Archer, *Massachusetts Historical Society Collections*, 3d Series, 8:74, 75.
40. The two 'inlets' which he saw between Nauset and Chatham were the openings into old Monomoyick (now Pleasant) Bay. One was the one I have described where the *Sparrowhawk* came in, and the other probably just north of the old Harbor Coast Guard Station, which has been open within the last fifty years.
41. *Voyages of Sieur de Champlain*, Prince Society Edition, 2:118.
42. *Ibid.*, 2:122. [Map faces 122 with explanation on 122.]
43. That is, although the main entrance to Pleasant Bay lay much farther north, the Bars were no doubt much the same about its mouth as Chatham Bars are at its mouth today.
44. Archer, *Massachusetts Historical Society Collections*, 3d Series, 8:74, 75.
45. Smith, *History of Chatham*, 2:209, 3:219. [Pages 209 and 280 as in bibliography]
46. What we know today as Monomoy Point is sometimes shown on early maps as Cape Malabar, a title borrowed from the French name for Nauset, just as we have borrowed the name Monomoy from the old name of the present Pleasant Bay and the Indian tribe who lived about it.
47. Blunt's *American Coast Pilot*, 187, 188.
48. Eldredge's *Coast Pilot*, No. 4.
49. Coast and Geodetic Survey chart, 1209.
50. Archer, *Massachusetts Historical Society Collections*, 3d Series, 8:74, 75.
51. Eldredge's *Coast Pilot*, No. 4:258.
52. It is interesting to note that this point, or its representative, has never gone by any other name than 'Sandy Point' in the local vernacular, from first to last.
53. *Voyages of Sieur de Champlain*, Prince Society Edition, 2:119.
54. Champlain gives the compass declination 18° 40′ west, at Nauset, in 1605. [81]
55. See maps of Champlain, Smith, the Dutch, Wood, Hubbard, Southack, etc.
56. Chart of 1723, including the Whida chart of 1717.
57. *Massachusetts Magazine*, 1790; Smith, *History of Chatham*, 1:11.
58. Otis, *New England Historical and Genealogical Register*, 18:37-44. [44]
59. Blunt's *American Coast Pilot*, 187, 188.
60. Morison, *Maritime History of Massachusetts*, back end map.
61. Eldredge's *Coast Pilot* No. 4:257. For previous dates also.
62. Personal correspondence.
63. Blunt's *American Coast Pilot*, 189.
64. *Ibid.*
65. The result of this inward drift is being exemplified today at Chatham, where the north point of the beach is deflecting the current in toward the land, and sweeping everything before it.
66. I have not gone into the details of the changes near Chatham itself, because they have little bearing on the passage of a ship bound over the Shoals. The subject is

well covered in the *History of Chatham*, by W. C. Smith, the best authority known. Suffice it to say that the changes here are constant and orderly, repeating over and over the same old program. The North Beach makes down to about opposite the Lights, James's Head undermines and recedes, then the harbor mouth blocks up with bars, and some heavy easterly breaks through the beach somewhere farther north, forming a new entrance, probably in one of the ancient ones. A new South Beach builds up outside Chatham, and remains until the new entrance has worked down to it again, when it is again cut away, and the same process is repeated over again. This has happened several times since the white man arrived, and will continue until the harbor becomes wholly choked with sand flats, as is gradually happening.

67. On the authority of Captain George B. Nickerson, of the Nauset Coast Guard Station.
68. Authority of Captain C. M. Tobin, of Pollack Lightship, No. 101.
69. Authority of Captain Francis E. Hammond, Pilot.

4

The Landfall and the Landing

We have been a long time wading up to the ninth of November, sixteen hundred and twenty, Old Style, but at last we have arrived. Without a general preliminary knowledge of our ship, her crew, and the coast she is to navigate, it would have been utterly useless for me or any one else to attempt to calculate her position. Perhaps that is why others have been contented to let it stand in its vagueness.

It has been my purpose to present a background of facts in the preceding pages, which, to me, seems necessary to an intelligent study of the day's works of the ninth, tenth, and eleventh. With this layout as a basis, we can now 'go on location,' as they say in the movies, and work out the details from the conditions we find as we go along.

In making my calculations as to the times of sunrise, sunset, lunar phases, tidal currents, etc., I have taken the word of the men who were there that it was on the ninth of November, 1620, O.S., when they first made the land. A few days one way or the other would make no material difference in the length of the day, but it would very materially affect the phase of the moon, and, conjointly, the hours and strengths of the tidal current.

Mourt's Relation, written by the participants soon after it occurred, says: 'upon the ninth of November' 'by breake of the day we espied land which wee deemed to be Cape Cod, and so afterward it proved.'[1] Bradford confirms the place of their landfall when he says: 'they fell with that land which is called Cape Cod; the which being made & certainly knowne to be it, they were not a little joyfull.'[2] He does not mention the date, however, and he mixes the issue a little when he goes on to say: 'And ye next day they gott into ye Cape-harbor wher they ridd in saftie.'[3] A little later he says: 'Being thus arrived at Cap-Cod ye 11. of November,'[4] which, coupled with his former statement that the next day after making the land they 'gott into ye Cape-Harbour,' would lead to the natural inference that it was on the tenth when they made the land.

Mourt's Relation, however, specifically states that it was the ninth when the land was sighted, and there is good reason to believe that it was Bradford himself who penned these lines in the Relation.[5] Both his History and the Relation agree that it was the eleventh when they anchored in Provincetown Harbor, and the date of the signing of the famous Compact, and the attendant circumstances connected with it,[6] prove it. In addition, a careful reading of the following pages will show that the *Mayflower* could not well have covered the track she did under the circumstances which she encountered, in much less time than the Relation gives her.

It is my opinion that Bradford, in compiling his history years after the events happened, meant to convey the idea that on 'ye next day' after sighting the land, they got up around the Head of the Cape into the safe waters of the Bay, which they unquestionably did, although it was not until the forenoon of the eleventh that they actually anchored inside of Long Point, in Provincetown Harbor. Read it any way you will, and the weight of the evidence is clearly for the ninth, as the day they made the land.

The thirteenth fell on a Monday, according to the Relation. That was the day the *Mayflower* women went ashore and inaugurated Monday as washday for future New England housewives.[7] Therefore the ninth must have been a Thursday; and so, from the evidence of people who were there, we have established the facts that the first land they saw was Cape Cod, that the date was Thursday, the ninth of November, and that the time was daybreak.

Daybreak is a very variable hour in this part of the world. Sunrise can be depended on to the minute, be the weather fair or foul, but there are so many elements entering into the time when daylight will break that the most weatherwise can no more than hazard a guess from one day to the next. Cloudy, threatening weather materially retards the daylight from coming up, and shortens the interval between daybreak and sunrise. A heavy night fog— no uncommon occurrence on this coast—has much the same effect. A clear, crisp morning, however, gives daybreak at the maximum interval before the rising of the sun, and even this is about a fifth shorter in November than in July.[8]

Bradford states distinctly that the weather was clear when he tells us that, after making sure what land they had sighted, 'they tacked aboute and resolved to stande for ye southward (ye wind & weather being fair).'[9] This evidence not only dispels any question as to the condition of the early morning weather, but also gives a very definite clue as to the direction of the wind at that time, which at this season of the year is a prime factor in determining whether the weather will be clear or cloudy.

There can be no question that, at the time they tacked about, they had been standing in from the eastward to satisfy themselves that it was the Cape they had made. There also can be no question but that Bradford, at the time he made this statement, was sailor enough to know what was meant by 'tacking about.'[10] Therefore, in order to have had a wind which obliged them to tack, and was a fair wind after they tacked ship and stood to the southward, the wind must have been from somewhere from between west and north. Had it been anywhere from between north and east, the *Mayflower* would have been running in with a fair wind when she made the land, and there would have been no necessity for tacking ship, as she did, to go to the southward. With the wind from this quarter, all Captain Jones would have had to do, after he had run in far enough to make sure of his landfall, would have been to slack his sheets and swing her off before the wind onto a southerly course. If the wind had been from between east and south, it could not have been 'faire' for a southward course after they 'tacked aboute,' as Bradford expressly says it was. The same answer applies to a wind from between south and west; and the fact that the wind came 'contrary,' or from the south, whither they were heading, along some time in the afternoon, proves conclusively that they had no southerly wind in the early part of the day.

This leaves no possible quadrant from which to look for the wind but between west and north, and I will narrow this down a little when I get to work on the different positions of the *Mayflower*. For the present purpose of establishing the state of weather at daybreak of the ninth, however, the fact that the wind was from the northwest quarter is sufficient, because in the month of November on Cape Cod this wind is invariably accompanied by the clearest of clear weather.

The course pursued by Captain Jones after he first made the land amply supports this conclusion. It is certain he never would have stood boldly in toward a strange coast in thick, hazy weather, nor with a threatening onshore wind from the eastward. Neither his ship nor his experience would warrant it. I might add that it was very fortunate for New England that it was clear when the *Mayflower* made Cape Cod, and that it continued so until she was safely anchored in Provincetown Harbor.

There seems, then, to be no reason to doubt that it was a clear, crisp morning, with a northwesterly breeze off the land, when daylight broke on this memorable day. The sun rose on the Back Side of the Cape that morning at very nearly 6:55 A.M.[11] The moon, which was nine days after full,[12] was hanging in mid-sky, a waning crescent, too thin to help much toward hurrying daybreak along. With these facts to base an opinion on, I asked the judgment of two extremely competent and intelligent men as to how long before sunrise day would break so that there would be light enough for a ship offshore a possible eight or ten miles to be able to make out the land.

One of these men is a fisherman who has spent his whole life off back of the Cape.[13] He has witnessed hundreds of days break right where the *Mayflower* sighted the land. He gave me as his opinion that day would break not over half an hour before the time of sunrise, at that season of the year and under the above conditions, so that there would be light enough to see the land from off some seven to ten miles, or just in 'the lay of the land,' as he calls it.

The other man is Captain of the Coast Guard Station at Nauset,[14] who tells me that the land at his station is visible from about twelve miles offshore under clear conditions, and could probably be seen about twenty minutes before sunrise, and thirty minutes after sunset, under conditions as they appear to have been when the *Mayflower* made the land.

I am confident there are no better judges of this question in the world. Incidentally, both these men have *Mayflower* blood enough almost to balance the salt water in their veins. Other local men of long experience in these waters, who, by the nature of their calling, observe these natural phenomena closely, corroborate the judgment of these two men.

This would fix the hour of daybreak, when the Pilgrims say they 'espied' the land, at twenty to thirty minutes before the time of sunrise, which was about six-fifty-five that morning. Thus we can add to our little nucleus of knowledge that it was about half-past six in the morning when the Pilgrims caught their first glimpse of the sands of Cape Cod over the bow of the *Mayflower;* that a thin slice of old moon about seven hours high [15] was hanging over the mastheads, with its horns pointing toward the land;[16] and that a land breeze from the northwest was the harbinger of a clear sunrise at five minutes of seven.

This, then, was the hour, and these the conditions, when those on the *Mayflower* espied the land which was to be their journey's end. But just where they were at daybreak, and just what particular part of the fifty-mile stretch of Back Side it was they espied, neither they themselves nor anyone since have ever told us. It is necessary, therefore, to work along until we can pick up some known landmark, and then work back from that to the hour of daybreak to see just where the *Mayflower* was at that time.

Not until shortly before dark, on the afternoon of that same day, do the *Mayflower* passengers give us accurate and definite information as to exactly where they were then. They had at that time reached the 'deangerous shoulds and roring breakers'[17] of the Shoals of Pollack Rip. This is the first position for the day of which we are absolutely sure from the records, and is the key to every other position both on this day and the next. By determining the hour of the *Mayflower*'s arrival here, we shall have not only a fixed landmark from which to work, but also a given hour, and can figure her day's work either forward or back with a great degree of accuracy. Not only that, but her subsequent courses and positions during the days of the tenth and eleventh are directly affected by the hour and place where she turned back on the ninth. Thanks to the records left by her passengers, we are able to calculate very closely the hour of her arrival on the Shoals.

Bradford tells us, that, after they had stood in and made certain what land it was, in the morning, they held a consultation among themselves and with Master Jones, and then tacked ship and stood to the southward, with a fair wind and good weather.

> But after they had sailed yt course aboute halfe ye day, they fell amongst deangerous shoulds and roring breakers, and they were so farr intangled ther with as they conceived them selves in great danger; & ye wind shrinking upon them withall, they resolved to bear up againe for the Cape, and thought them selves hapy to gett out of those dangers before night overtooke them, as by Gods providence they did.[18]

Mourt's Relation tells us much the same story, adding the information that after they tacked to the southward in the morning, 'wee made our course South South West, purposing to goe to a River ten leagues to the South of the Cape, but at night the winde being contrary, we put round againe for the Bay of Cape Cod.'[19]

It is plain from these records that the *Mayflower* had been sailing a 'South South West'[20] course 'about halfe ye day' when she arrived at the Shoals. By 'halfe ye day' is undoubtedly meant half the daylight hours of the late autumn day. The sun rose about 6:55 A.M. on this particular day, and set about 4:35 P.M.[21] That a half-hour of daylight before sunrise and another half-hour after sunset would be about all of daylight that can reasonably be allowed, has already been shown, making a total of ten and a half daylight hours for the day. At the outside, about half a day's sailing time could not have been over six hours, and in my opinion is plenty to allow. Therefore, the time which had elapsed from the time the *Mayflower* 'tacked aboute' and stood on her south-south-west course until she became snarled up amongst the Shoals, was approximately six hours.

Bradford says that after their arrival at the Shoals the wind moderated on them while they were among the rips, and that they were thankful to get out from amongst them and back into deep water again before night shut down, 'as by Gods providence they did.' [22] Mourt's Relation says that they 'put round againe,' or headed back from the Shoals 'at night the winde being contrary.' [23] From the two versions it is evident that it was pretty well along toward night when the *Mayflower* got clear of the Shoals and headed north again. From this premise, let us see about how long a ship of the *Mayflower*'s capabilities might be in disentangling herself from the entrance to the Shoals, under the conditions which she found there on the afternoon of the ninth of November. By referring to the map her relative position will become clear.

There can be no reasonable doubt that she was down in the neighborhood of what is known today as the Broken Part of Pollack Rip when she got mixed up in the Shoals and hauled back. I have explained my general reasons for this in my section of this paper devoted to the Back Side. Following a south-south-west course down by Chatham, and leaving what was then Gilbert's Point about two miles on the starboard beam, in ten fathoms of water, would bring the *Mayflower* first into nine, then into eight, then seven, and lastly into six fathoms of water,[24] with not much to worry about. Old Cape Batturier, which is now marked by Bearse's Shoal, would be about a mile and a half to starboard, and it would look like plain sailing ahead to anyone unfamiliar with this locality.

At this time of day the tide would be setting out over the Shoals in a northeasterly directly at a velocity of perhaps one and a half to two knot speed.[25] As the wind was 'shrinking withall' and soon came 'contrary'—that is, from the southward—it is obvious that the *Mayflower* could not have been making over a mile an hour, at this time, with the tide against her and very light winds, even if fair. In spite of her slow headway, she would suddenly find herself in shoal water, for a ship comes on to the northeast edge of the Shoals pretty abruptly. At that period there is little doubt that there were many bars here which ebbed out dry at low water, and would disclose themselves only at half-tide by 'roring breakers.' The *Mayflower* must have stumbled right in among these, and with a loaded ship drawing twelve feet of water, a baffling wind or none at all with which to keep steerage way on her, and a two-knot tide sweeping her hither and yon across these shifting sands, Captain Jones was in one of the tightest boxes he had ever been, I can assure you, and no doubt he realized it.

The sun was rapidly drawing down to nightfall. He had to act, and that quickly. He knew it was no place to anchor his ship for the night, except as a last resort. The rising of the swell, the coming on of a storm, or even ebbing of the tide might pound the bottom out of his ship. The only other alternative was to run the risk of getting her aground in working her back into deep water while daylight lasted. He took that chance; and I pause to compliment the consummate skill and seamanship of the Master of the *Mayflower* in extricating his ship from this extremely perilous situation without a scratch. So will any sailor who has had any experience in a tub of an old windjammer under similar circumstances.

The Broken Part of Pollack Rip is one of the meanest stretches of shoal water on the American Coast, and was none the less so in 1620. Had not the 'faire wind' which had brought him down to the Shoals changed to the south and come 'contrary' at just the psychological moment when he was snarled up among the 'deangerous shoulds and roring breakers,' giving him a chance to make a fair wind of it in clawing back again into deep water, he could hardly have done it, neither by 'Gods providence' nor otherwise. Champlain pounded down over this same 'very dangerous place' only a few years previously, in a ship drawing only four feet of water, striking bottom and damaging his ship, all because he had the wind to the north and could not get back. With a loaded ship drawing twelve feet, it is altogether probable that Captain Jones could not possibly have saved his ship from shivering her timbers on the Shoals of Pollack Rip, if not laying her bones there for good and all, had not the wind changed as it did.

That the *Mayflower* got in on to the Shoals far enough so that all hands 'conceived themselves in great danger' is certain. That they did not get clear until the wind changed in their favor 'at night' is what we gather from their own words,[26] and anyone at all familiar with the Shoals or with handling square-rigged ships will know that this must be so. Under these circumstances, it is reasonable to conclude that she must have entered in among the shoals at least a quarter to a half-mile—she would almost do that before her master was aware of the danger. Fifteen or twenty minutes would be all that would be necessary to carry him this distance, from comparative safety into dire extremity. Then, with his ship becalmed or nearly so, another fifteen or twenty minutes could easily be consumed in floundering around among the rips. If he worked her out through this mess in less than another twenty minutes after he caught the fair wind from the southward, he was lucky, even with a fair tide.

Altogether, an hour is a conservative allowance to make for the period which elapsed from the time the *Mayflower* first came on to the Shoals until she had sounded her way out again into safe water. Another hour, before a freshening southerly wind, and a two-knot tide pushing under her counters, would take her out through the best of the water on about an east-north-east course, and into fifteen or twenty fathoms of water 'before night overtook them.'[27] A total of two hours in all is probably a fair estimate of the elapsed time from her arrival at the Shoals to the hour of nightfall, and it could not possibly have been much less.

As I have said, the sun set about four-thirty-five on the night of the ninth. Night would overtake them by five o'clock, and would shut down with a bang, there being no moon to stretch the twilight out.[28] Therefore, the hour of the *Mayflower*'s arrival at the Shoals must have been about three o'clock in the afternoon, or two hours before nightfall. This gives us an hour not far from correct, and a definite landmark from which to take a departure in calculating either way, forward or back.

The *Mayflower* had been sailing on a south-south-west course about six hours, or 'halfe ye day,' when she arrived at the Shoals at approximately three o'clock on the afternoon of the ninth of November, 1620. Therefore, six hours back along this course should bring us, at nine o'clock in the morning, to the position she was in when she 'tacked aboute' and stood to the southward, after standing in since daybreak to make sure what land it was she had sighted. In order to determine with any degree of accuracy how many miles she covered in that six hours, it is necessary to calculate as nearly as possible what she met with in the way of wind and tide, and apply their effects to her known sailing ability.

As the wind was the determining factor in both her tacking to the south in the morning, and again in her hauling back from the shoals in the afternoon, I will consider that element first.

In proving that daylight rose clear on the morning of the ninth, I showed that no other wind than one from the west to north quarter would admit of the known facts that after standing in to make sure of her landfall, the *Mayflower* tacked ship on to a south-south-west course and made a fair wind of it. A glance at my map of the Back Side showing the track of the *Mayflower* will make this perfectly obvious to anyone at all familiar with handling sailing ships.

Bradford clearly states, as I have already quoted, that the wind was fair while they were running down the Back Side to the Shoals. The Relation says that they turned back at night, the wind being contrary, which can only mean that up to late afternoon they had held a favorable wind. Bradford adds that while they were negotiating the Shoals, the wind was shrinking upon them. Taken in the entirety, the description of the wind as left to us by the Pilgrims proves conclusively that the westerly wind on which they had stood in toward the land after daybreak had become northerly and 'faire' when they tacked to the south, and had continued to be a free wind up until nearly night, when it came in from the southward.

From this premise, it seems practically certain that the ninth of November was the kind of day which is common on Cape Cod at this season of the year. It is usually preceded by one or two days of strong northwesterly winds, and followed by a day or two of southerlies. Such a day, coming on the 'tail end of a Norther,' is known to Cape-Codders as a 'sea-turn day'—I suppose because the wind turns around by the seaward gauge, rather than by the landward. On a sea-turn day the changes of the wind can be depended upon, and forecast almost with the certainty with which the cycle of a hurricane is reckoned by seamen. It is invariably accompanied by some of the most beautiful days of the year, a sort of late Indian Summer, when Nature seems to pause awhile for breath, before pitching into winter in dead earnest. Every move of the *Mayflower* on this day, as well as on the two subsequent days bears out this supposition.

It is probable that at daybreak the wind was off the land, and well to the westward. As the sun got up, and the *Mayflower* worked in under the land, it hauled more to the northward and headed her off, about coincident with the time of the high-water slack. Very likely this was the reason she tacked to the southward at nine o'clock as much as anything else, because I believe Captain Jones would have made for Provincetown Harbor then and there, if the chances had been favorable. Up to the time the sun turned at noon, the wind would be likely to continue from the northward, a good leading breeze, and after that to swing out more to the eastward and moderate, until by the time she had arrived at the Shoals at three o'clock, the fair wind would be pretty well played out. The next sequence on such a day would be to expect the wind to breeze up from the southward and this is just what it did. This is not a mere fanciful arrangement of mine to suit the case, but is based on a knowledge of the usual turns of the wind on such a day as the people who were there tell us they had.

I have already shown that the normal sailing speed of the *Mayflower* was about two and one half knots an hour, taking it by and large. With everything in her favor, she was capable of four or better. So I believe I am allowing her plenty when I give her an average speed *through the water* of four miles an hour for the first three hours of her south-south-west course, and possibly for the fourth hour, or the hour from 12 M. to 1 P.M. Considering her load, the condition of her bottom, and all the other factors on which I have already touched in my study of the ship herself, this seems to me very liberal, even with a good breeze and a fair wind.

After 1 P.M., the wind would certainly be 'shrinking upon them withall'; and while her sails would be drawing better as the wind went out to the eastward, her speed would slacken proportionately as the wind did. Three miles *through the water* for the hour from 1 to 2 P.M. would be about all I should expect of her.

For the last hour, from 2 to 3 P.M., the wind would moderate still more, but being 'full and by,' with the wind well to the eastward, she might *log* a couple of miles in that last hour.

This would bring her to the Shoals at 3 P.M. with a total of twenty-one miles logged since 9 A.M. on a south-south-west course; but before we can lay the parallel rulers down on the chart and prick a position twenty-one miles north-north-east from the Broken Part of Pollack Rip as her nine o'clock position, we must apply the effect of the tidal currents to every hour of the six. On account of the peculiarities of the tides in this region, there seems to be no other way to do this accurately than by working back hour by hour from her known position at the Shoals at 3 P.M., and adding or subtracting the velocity of the tidal current, as the case may be, to her logged speed through the water.

In making this calculation I make no allowance for possible delays in making soundings, which was undoubtedly frequently done, because at the slow gait she was going through the water, the hand-lead could be used by an experienced hand without checking her speed. I have also assumed that the tidal currents were not appreciably different in 1620 from the present, my study of the changes in the configuration of the coast and shoals showing nothing to affect radically either the direction or the strength of the tides. I use the words 'miles' and 'knots' interchangeably, as I was taught aboardship, but in either case and always in this paper I refer to the nautical mile of this particular locality, as shown on the charts of the Coast and Geodetic Survey.

It was high tide at Nauset about nine o'clock in the forenoon of November ninth.[29] This would mean a tidal current at Pollack Rip Shoals at three o'clock in the afternoon setting about north-north-east, or practically right ahead for the *Mayflower* when she arrived there. There is ordinarily a full strength current there of from one and a half to two miles an hour, even increasing to three and a half miles at times on the full of the moon. As the moon was small, only four days before new, and the weather mild and settled,[30] I should judge the velocity of the tides was rather weak. During the hour previous to three o'clock the *Mayflower* had not quite arrived at the Shoals, and the tide had not quite got going in its full strength; therefore, a conservative ratio of one mile an hour head tide seems logical, which, deducted from her speed of two miles an hour *through the water*, leaves one mile of actual ground covered from 2 to 3 P.M.

For the hour from 1 to 2 P.M. she would be just getting down into the head tide in good shape, and an allowance of a half-knot tide against her is a fair estimate. This, taken from her logged speed of three miles, leaves her an actual mileage of two miles and a half for this hour.

The hour from 12 M. to 1 P.M. would find her running out of her fair tide she had carried all the morning, pushing through the slack and into a tide turning against her. A half-mile setback of tidal current against her four miles logged would be large, leaving her an actual mileage of three and a half miles this hour.

Thus far, her actual corrected mileage for this three hours back from the Shoals has been seven miles, and places her at twelve o'clock noon about three miles due east from Chatham. It being high tide at Nauset at 9 A.M. this day, and allowing until nine-thirty for the end of the highwater slack, the tide would continue to run south down by Chatham until twelve o'clock noon, or after.

Still continuing on the back track for the hour from 11 A.M. to noon, we have a favoring tide of about a half knot to add to her four miles logged, giving her an actual mileage of four and a half miles. During the hour between 10 and 11 A.M. the tide is still more favorable, a one-knot current pushing her along in addition to her own four miles, and making a maximum of five miles actually covered in this hour.

Another hour of partly slack water and partly fair tide gives her a possible half-mile to add to her four miles logged, and places her at 9 A.M. in a position twenty-one miles north-north-east from the Broken Part of Pollack Rip and five and one half miles east by south from the South Wellfleet beach near the site of the old Marconi Station.

This, then, is the place where the *Mayflower* lay, while the Pilgrims and the Master consulted as to the best course to pursue, now that they were sure the land they had made was Cape Cod. Here is where she 'tacked aboute' on the morning of the ninth of November, 1620, and started on her 'South South West' course for 'aboute halfe ye day.' No other position on the Back Side of Cape Cod answers to all the requirements called for by the facts as recorded by the men who were there at the time. No other position coincides with calculations based on a knowledge of the principles of navigation as applied to such a ship as the *Mayflower,* under the conditions of wind, weather, and tides such as we know she met with.

This position is near enough to the beach so that the wooded hills back of the shore-line could be readily seen, as they are described by the passengers. It is offshore far enough for Captain Jones to make a south-south-west course clear of Chatham Bars to the Shoals of Pollack Rip—a course which has not been improved on in three hundred years, for sailing ships. It is far enough south so that the *Mayflower* could reach the Shoals in about half a day's sail with average winds and tides. And last, but by no means least, it is far enough north so that men on her decks, who were somewhat familiar with the coast, could make out unmistakably that one distinguishing landmark of Cape Cod, the Highland of Truro.

The bold clay bluffs south of where Highland Light stands today, rising nearly one hundred and fifty feet sheer from the sea,[31] would be plainly visible from the decks of the *Mayflower*, bearing northwest, less than eleven miles distant.[32] Stretching south from there along the Wellfleet shore to almost abeam of the *Mayflower*'s position, the high banks of the Back Side, more than a hundred feet high in many places, would make the identification certain to any sailor who had ever seen the Cape before. Master's Mates Clark and Coppin had both been in these waters, perhaps more than once, and the Highland of Cape Cod once seen is never confused with any other landmark on the North American coast.

That this nine o'clock position is approximately correct is proved by its standing the test of every known requirement. It even measures up to the description given by the Pilgrims of the land they first saw as 'a goodly land,' 'wooded to the brink of the sea.' Neither the hundred-foot cliffs of the Clay Pounds at Truro nor the sandy stretches of the Monomoy beaches would quite warrant that description, even in 1620. If I have erred, it is in overestimating the speed of the *Mayflower*, or underestimating the eyesight of her officers; for were it not that it seems that this position must necessarily have been far enough to the north so that her officers could make out the Highland clearly, I would place her even farther south at this time.

As it is, this position will have to stand as the place where the *Mayflower* 'tacked aboute,' until someone who knows more about it than I do rises up with proof to the contrary. It adds one more milestone to the day's work of the ninth, and brings us that much nearer to her position at daybreak, two and a half hours earlier, when she first sighted the Back Side of Cape Cod.

They tell us in Mourt's Relation,[33] that at daybreak, when they sighted the land, they 'deemed' it 'to be Cape Cod, and so afterward it proved.' They also add how pleased they were to see it wooded to the brink of the sea.

Bradford [34] explains that they 'fell with that land which is called Cape Cod, the which being made and certainly known to be it, they wer not a little joyfull.' After it was 'certainly known,' they held a 'deliberation' 'amongst themselves and with ye mr. of ye ship,' and finally 'tacked aboute' 'to stand to the southward.'

From their own story, as quoted above, it is evident that when they first saw the land at daybreak, they were not near enough to be absolutely sure what land it was. Obviously, they had to stand in toward the land some way before it was 'certainly known' to be Cape Cod, as 'afterward it proved.'

Being convinced beyond the question of a doubt that they had got hold of the Cape, the next thing was to decide on their future course. Their present necessity of getting ashore somewhere was beginning to be of equal, if not greater, importance than that of carrying out their original plan of getting south to the region of the Hudson. An hour might easily have been consumed in debating this momentous question. No doubt Captain Jones backed his main-topsail and hove his ship to, while he discussed matters with his passengers; but the wind favoring them for a southward course while the discussion was under way, in the end they 'tacked aboute' and stood to the 'South South West.'

While the *Mayflower* was lying hove-to, her position would not materially change, except for a slight drift one way or the other, the tide still setting toward the north in this locality, and the wind now coming from well to the north. Therefore, assuming that an hour may have been spent in the 'deliberation,' her eight o'clock position where she hove-to would be the same as that from which she tacked ship to the southward at 9 A.M. This would give her an actual sailing time of very near one hour and a half to bring her in from her daybreak position at 6:30 to her nine o'clock position five and a half miles east by south from the old Marconi Station on South Wellfleet beach.

As I have before shown, the fact that she tacked ship at 9 A.M. and made a fair wind of it on a south-south-west course, proves conclusively that she had been heading in toward the land in a northwesterly direction when 'it proved' to be Cape Cod. There is no other wind but a westerly wind at sunrise, hauling more to the northward as the sun got up and the *Mayflower* worked in under the land, that can possibly fit to these facts. Therefore, she must have been close-hauled on the port tack, with the flood tide pushing her to windward, during the hour and a half she was standing in toward the land from 6:30 until 8 A.M. Close-hauled on the wind was not her fast point of sailing, and I do not see how she could have covered more than five miles in the whole hour and a half, or made good a course of better than northwest by north.

If, therefore, we follow back about five miles along the northwest by north course which brought her in to her nine o'clock position, we should arrive at 6:30 A.M., or daybreak of the ninth of November, 1620, O.S., at the spot where the *Mayflower* was when the Pilgrims first saw the land.

This position, the one above all others which has haunted me with its vagueness, lies nearly east by south from the Nauset Coast Guard Station in Eastham, about nine miles offshore; and about the same distance east by north from the beach at East Orleans where the town road leads down to the Back Side near the Mayo Duck Farm.

The location of this position, which cannot be very far from right, ought to be of interest to every *Mayflower* descendant. Here our ancestors caught their first glimpse of their promised land, a land which they were to dedicate in suffering and privation to a posterity of sturdy citizenry. Here, some of them beheld for the first time the very hills which were to be their earthly heritage while life should last, and their eternal resting-place when their little course was run. Here, in the golden sunrise of a beautiful November morning, their souls must have risen to heights such as are seldom attained in the range of human emotions. No stone can ever mark the spot where the Back Side first opened out on the tear-dimmed, joyful eyes of the Pilgrims, yet it may be that the sunbeams will fall a little softer there, and the breezes touch the waves a little more tenderly, because of them.

It is quite generally supposed that the *Mayflower* hit upon Cape Cod by accident. I am sure this is not so. The fact that the Pilgrims felt reasonably sure the land they saw at daybreak was Cape Cod is proof enough that some one knew what land it ought to be. Of their own knowledge, the Pilgrims themselves could not have guessed whether it was Cape Cod or Fire Island. They were neither sailors nor navigators, and aside from one or two members of their company,[35] there is no likelihood that any of them had ever laid eyes on the American Continent before. Two of the ship's officers[36] had been in this locality previously, but it would take something more definite than that to account for the Pilgrims believing it was the Cape they had made, until they had stood in far enough to make it out clearly. The logical answer is that the navigating officer of the *Mayflower,* Captain Christopher Jones, knew that he was close to the forty-second parallel of north latitude, and was heading in toward Cape Cod to make it, when they sighted the land.

That he was headed in toward the land at the time he tacked to the southward is certain, and there is nothing in the record to show that he had changed his course since daylight, up to this time. He was only a very few miles south of 42°, and it would seem from the known facts that he was doing the best he could, with the wind and tide he had, to get back on to that parallel. It was an old established custom of the early navigators to strike the latitude of the place they wished to make, and then run for it on that parallel. He was not especially anxious to make Cape Cod, but conditions beyond his control were getting to such extremity that he must have been exceedingly anxious to get hold of *terra firma* somewhere, and soon.

He had been held back by all kinds of bad weather and other exasperating causes until winter was shutting in on him. With a sprung main beam his ship was in no fit condition to buck heavy weather. Fresh water was getting scarce,[37] fresh provisions were running low, they were all out of firewood.[38] Scurvy was breaking out among crew and passengers, and the stork was due to come aboard again for the second time almost any day now. Any clear-headed shipmaster in Captain Jones's shoes would have hauled in for the nearest land when he got a favorable break, and, once he was sure he had hold of it in good shape, do the next best thing with whatever wind and weather the Lord provided him at that time.

It is very certain that Captain Jones had had clear northwest winds for a day or two before the ninth. With a good noon sight of the sun on these two days, or even on the eighth alone, his old 'hog-yoke' would tell him that he was down to the forty-second parallel of latitude, which he knew perfectly well would lead him in to Cape Cod if he followed it in. He could not have depended on his longitude position, having had no way to check up his dead reckoning since leaving England, and was probably wondering why he had not already made westing enough to raise the land, the Gulf Stream current being sufficient to upset even the shrewdest calculations of a past-master at dead reckoning. But he was sure of his latitude, and finding himself close to the forty-second parallel, and the weather conditions wholly in his favor for working in toward the land, it is likely that that is just what he was doing.

He must have known he was pretty well in toward the Cape before daylight of the ninth, whether he so confided to his passengers or not. He must have got bottom on soundings, by daybreak at least, to be near enough in to see the land, although it is extremely doubtful if he would let his ship get into much less than seventy-five fathoms before it was light enough to see. He must have known on the day before, by the change in the color of the sea water and by the general appearance of the western clouds, that the land was not far off; and it is more than likely he had already caught the pungent, earthy smell of the land in the offshore breeze. Landsmen may not appreciate that to a mariner approaching the coast after long days at sea, a wind from off the land is as laden with the message of the earth and growing things as ever the sea breeze is of things salty to the nose of the landlubber.

That Captain Jones was reasonably sure he had made Cape Cod, even before he got in close enough so that his men who had seen it before could identify it, seems evident. That he was making as near a west course along the forty-second parallel of north latitude as the conditions would allow, also seems certain. The fact that we find him just at daylight in about seventy-five fathoms of water, with the land just in sight, is no accident, but the logical result of a common-sense course such as we should expect of Captain Christopher Jones.

With the position of the *Mayflower* at daybreak of the ninth worked out as nine miles east by south of the Nauset Coast Guard Station, with her track pricked out from there in until she tacked about at 9 A.M., five and one-half miles east by south of the old Marconi Station on the South Wellfleet shore, and with her south-south-west course corrected to the Shoals, let us see where it is likely she spent the remainder of the daylight hours of the ninth, after she got back into safe water again off somewhere southeast of Chatham.

When she came running down from the north-north-east at 3 P.M., she had a fair or quartering wind to push her in on to the Shoals against a one and one-half or two-knot current. Coincident with her getting messed up on the Broken Part of Pollack Rip, the fair wind died down, and a wind from the southward sprang up, as I have already explained. This enabled her to scrabble out of the bad pocket she was in and get back into deep water before night overtook her.

We need not doubt but that Captain Jones fully realized the danger he had just escaped, and his sailor's judgment would tell him to lose no time, now that he had wind and tide in his favor, in giving both the Shoals and the mainland north of it as wide a berth as possible while he could see to run. It had undoubtedly taken him all of an hour to sound his way out into seven fathoms of water, a mile or so to the northeast of the Shoals, and with sunset at four-thirty-five, it would be getting dark by five o'clock. This gave him not over an hour in which to make an offing, and I will wager he drove the old *Mayflower* for every ounce that was in her while the daylight lasted. Keeping her right in the best of the water with everything drawing alow and aloft, and with a two-knot tide kicking her right in the stern, she may have covered five miles before it got too dark to see to run. This would put her about six miles to the east-north-east of the Shoals by five o'clock, and just about three miles east by north of the present location of Pollack Lightship 110, where she would have fifteen fathoms of water under her keel, and Chatham, the nearest land, northwest by west eight miles distant.

With night shutting down on him fast, with no chart to hint at what might lie ahead, with no moon till after midnight to lighten his path, and with his recent vivid illustration of how suddenly a ship might run into shoal water in this locality fresh in his mind, the logical thing to do would be to heave her to for the night.

These old-timers did not anchor in much over fifteen fathoms of water, as long as they had plenty of sea room and could hold their ground by heaving to. Captain Jones was deepening his water all the time, the wind and the tide were setting him away from the Shoals, and unless he was foolhardy enough to attempt to make a run for the Bay of Cape Cod through the utter darkness of an unlighted and dangerous coast with which he was wholly unacquainted, the only reasonable thing to do would be to heave to and hold his ground until he again had daylight to run by.

There is nothing in his record to suggest that he was rash or foolhardy, while on the contrary his whole course bespeaks a very shrewd and level-headed shipmaster, and I am so certain of what he would do under the circumstances that I am going to leave the *Mayflower* hove-to right here for the night of Thursday the ninth.

Thus ends the eventful daylight hours of the first day the Pilgrims ever spent on the American coast.

The Pilgrims left very little on record to enlighten us as to how they covered that fifty-mile stretch of water between the Shoals and Provincetown. About all they assure us of is that they were close to the Shoals at dark on Thursday the ninth, and that it took them from then until the forenoon of Saturday the eleventh to work the *Mayflower* from there around into Provincetown and get her anchor down. When I get to the day's work of Saturday the eleventh, I will show that it was probably well along in the forenoon when she did finally anchor; but in the mean time she had been some forty-odd hours somewhere off the Back Side of Cape Cod between the Shoals and Provincetown.

In leaving her hove-to for the night of the ninth, I stated my reasons for believing that Captain Jones would not attempt to run his ship very far on this coast during the hours of darkness. In circumstances such as he was in, it was not customary among navigators to take such undue risks unless driven to it by stress of weather, which he most certainly was not. This reasoning holds equally good for the night of the tenth; and all the time after daylight on the morning of the eleventh was unquestionably needed for working the *Mayflower* into Provincetown from some point near by, and for locating the best anchorage.

On this hypothesis, which is the only logical one and has been subjected to the expert criticism of experienced shipmasters, there only remain the daylight hours of Friday the tenth as actual sailing time in which to bring the *Mayflower* up from the Shoals to a position off the Head of the Cape near enough to Provincetown to slip into harbor as soon as it was light enough to see on the morning of the eleventh. This gives only about eleven hours, at most, in which to cover practically the whole distance.

As I have already said, a couple of days of southerly wind is usually expected to follow a sea-turn day, such as it seems almost certain the ninth had been. The arrival of the *Mayflower* in Provincetown Harbor as soon as the morning of the eleventh is proof positive that this was the quarter from which she had the wind. The Pilgrims themselves record that it was southerly late in the afternoon of the ninth; and that it continued so, until it had brought the *Mayflower* to within pretty close touch with Provincetown, is certain, otherwise she could hardly have reached there from the Shoals in forty *days*, let alone the forty *hours* it did take her.

It was an old maxim among coastwise sailormen that no sailing ship could beat to windward up by the Cape with the tide against her. While this was not absolutely true of every type of ship, it was literally true of ships of the *Mayflower*'s vintage. Owing to the peculiar split of the tides off Nauset, it so happened that the *Mayflower* managed to hold a head tide nearly all day of the tenth, as I shall presently show. For the present, the fact that she did buck the current most of the way around the Cape, and did make it in this comparatively short time, proves without a question of doubt that she held a southerly wind most of the time. It is also certain that, had the wind again changed to the north before Captain Jones was sure of getting around to the north of the Cape, he would have swung her off to the southward again, which would have been the line of least resistance.

A personal experience of my own well illustrates the futility of an old-time merchantman trying to get to the north, by the Cape, against the wind. I was once on board a square-rigged ship just east of the *Mayflower*'s position on the Shoals, having run up from Hatteras before a howling sou'wester of fog and rain. The girls in Boston seemed to be pulling the strings, and we picked up the Nantucket South Shoal Lightship about nine o'clock at night and shaped a course for Nauset with every expectation of being in the next day, after fifty-three days at sea without sight of land. In less than no time the wind flattened out, the glass took a nose-dive, and the next we knew we were headed out across George's in a screaming nor'wester. It was ten days later before we ever sighted the land, and then we made it at Cape Ann and never saw Cape Cod at all. We could smell it plainly enough at the time the wind struck off the land, but that was as near as we ever got to it.

We have, then, these premises to figure from in working the *Mayflower* north from the Shoals. We know her relative position at dark on the night of the ninth of November, and we also know that at this time she had a southerly wind. According to any reasonable logic based on the accumulated experience of seafaring men, she was then hove-to for the night; and by the same token, she must have held the southerly wind all of the next day, the tenth. At daylight of the eleventh, she was near enough to Provincetown to make it possible to get in during the fore part of the day, as I shall later demonstrate from the records. The tidal currents can be calculated very closely, knowing the age of the moon and the time of high water, and these I shall apply to her course hour by hour as we work to the northward. Thus, after all, we have quite an array of facts at hand to apply to what we already know we can expect the *Mayflower* herself to contribute.

At five o'clock, on the night of Thursday the ninth, when darkness shut down on the *Mayflower,* she should have been about six miles east-north-east of the Shoals, eight miles southeast by south from Chatham, and in about seventeen fathoms of water. The tide here would be running about east-north-east, perhaps at a knot an hour velocity. The wind was from the south, with probably some westerly in it, most likely about south-south-west, judging not only from what the Pilgrims say about it coming 'contrary' to their 'South South West' course—which is only a general term—but from the fact that after a mild sea-turn day that is about the direction to look for it from, with a northern tide running.

Under these conditions, Captain Jones would be likely to heave his ship to on the port tack, headed in, in order to head the tide as much as possible. She would lie about six points off from the wind, heading about west, and making good a course of about northeast as long as she held the northern tide.

By six o'clock this tide would be pretty well done, and she would be a mile or so to the northeast of her five o'clock position, still keeping in about seventeen fathoms depth, and on the port tack. For the next hour, during the slack and turn of the tide, she would just about hold her ground, and Captain Jones would have nothing to worry about. It would be a good time to get a snack to eat and have a quiet smoke, about the first opportunity I have seen for the Captain to catch his breath since he came down onto the Shoals after dinner.

After seven o'clock, with the tide making west-south-west, almost in the direction the *Mayflower* was heading, she would commence to range to the westward rather rapidly, so that by eight o'clock she would have made a west course of a mile or more and be getting into fifteen fathoms of water, or less. If the wind was light, which it is ten chances to one it was during the night, the Master of the *Mayflower* could now swing her off before the wind, with nothing but the spritsail on her, lee-bow the tide and make about a north-east course, a little better than holding his own.

By midnight, he would work a mile and a half or two miles out toward the twenty-fathom edge and into about eighteen fathoms of water; and with the moon rising about 12:20 A.M., to give him a little light to see by, he would feel fairly safe again.

The tide would start to the east-north-east once more by one o'clock, and he would have to let the *Mayflower* come up to the wind again in order not to go off over the edge with the tide. Heading about west, with the tide on her weather bow, he could now let her range ahead or fall back to suit his convenience, sagging along the twenty-fathom curve to the northwest, and making about half a mile an hour, or better.[39] At six o'clock in the morning he would be very near to where the whistling buoy is now located (1929-30), about five miles and a half due east from Chatham Light.

To anyone but a seaman, it may seem that I indulge in a great deal of speculation in logging the positions of the *Mayflower* through the night of the ninth. While of necessity this is true in a certain sense, every calculation is based on what I know would be the logical sequence of events for such a ship as the *Mayflower*, under the circumstances of wind and weather such as all the known facts indicate, and with conditions of tide which I know obtained in this locality on that night.

There are three excellent reasons for assuming that Captain Jones would hang off and on to the twenty-fathom edge through the night. The first is that he would not be likely to anchor as long as the weather was clear and mild, and he could keep his ship pretty close on to these soundings. The second is that here he would feel reasonably safe from suddenly running up into shoal water, as he had done once already on that day. The third is that the twenty-fathom hand-lead, rather than the heavier 'dipsy,' was the customary instrument used by the old-timers with which to keep track of their ships when hove-to, or reaching off and on, with the land close aboard and the water not too bold. At one cast of the lead a good leadsman would learn not only the kind of bottom he was on, but the depth of water, the direction of the drift of his ship and her speed, and the direction and strength of the tide. This may seem quite a mouthful to the uninitiated, but is wholly true, nevertheless.

By six o'clock of the morning of Friday the tenth, daylight would be streaking up in the east, and Captain Jones could begin to get the duck on the *Mayflower*. By the time he got everything on her and sheeted home, it would be light enough to see Chatham, which from this distance, with the daylight striking full on the eastern shore, would be seen distinctly by half-past six, if not before. He would then swing her off to the north along the twenty-fathom curve, with the tide making ahead, and probably with very light airs from the southward at this early hour in the morning. It is unlikely that he would make more than a mile and a half of northing before the sun rose at six-fifty-five. This would bring him to a position four miles east of the Old Harbor Coast Guard Station at seven o'clock.

After sunrise, the breeze would freshen, but the tide would be stronger as well, setting him back nearly a mile an hour against a possible three miles logged, so that two miles on a north course is enough to allow for the hour from seven to eight. Still sounding along in eighteen to twenty fathoms of water on a due north course for another hour, with the breeze getting a little stronger and the tide slacking a little as he worked to the north, would fetch him at nine o'clock where he would have Pochet Highlands bearing west, about three miles distant, having logged three miles and a half through the water and lost a half-mile by the head tide.

As the sun got up, the breeze would increase, and with the weather clear and the coastline ahead plainly visible, Captain Jones could crack it on to her, with the bonnets on the sails and everything drawing. Making good his due north course, and keeping pretty close to the 'edge,' four miles logged and a half-knot current against him would push him three miles and a half to the north in this hour, bringing Nauset Coast Guard Station due west at ten o'clock, and with eighteen fathoms of water two miles and a half from the beach.

This ten o'clock position of the tenth is very nearly on a line with the *Mayflower*'s position at daylight on the day before, when she first sighted the land, but six miles and a half nearer the beach.

She would catch the high-water slack along about here, but, being bound north, would meet the ebb, or southern, tide making against her as soon as she passed Nauset. From daylight in the morning of this day until nearly sunset in the afternoon, she was just in time to keep in the southern tide and buck it the whole length of the Back Side. As I have already stated, this is proof positive she must have had a fair wind.

From ten o'clock in the forenoon until two in the afternoon, a south-westerly wind is almost certain to be at its maximum strength, in this neighborhood, in a spell of mild weather. During this same period the *Mayflower* would hold an average of about a half-knot tide against her. Therefore, I have figured three and a half miles per hour of actual ground covered during this four hours, and simply note the courses steered and the landmarks passed from hour to hour.

Just after ten o'clock, while passing Nauset, Captain Jones would find that the north course, which had kept him in about twenty fathoms of water all the morning, was taking him on to shoaler ground, and he would haul her offshore a point, to north by east, which by eleven o'clock would bring him back on to the 'edge' again. He would be very near the position from which he tacked to the south on the previous day, being two and one half miles nearer the beach, and having the site of the old Marconi Station at South Wellfleet bearing west by north, three miles distant.

About here he would haul up to north by west, one half west, to keep his depth, and another hour would bring him at twelve o'clock noon into nineteen fathoms of water, with Cahoon's Hollow Coast Guard Station bearing west, two and three quarters miles distant. One o'clock would bring Pamet Coast Guard Station west by south, distant two miles and a half; and having nineteen fathoms of water, and, finding it growing deeper, he would change his course to northwest by north, one half north, which would carry him at two o'clock abreast of Highland Light. The present site of this world-famous lighthouse would bear west southwest, two and a half miles distant, and the *Mayflower* would have twenty fathoms of water under her keel.

Under the weather conditions which the *Mayflower* appears to have had this day, the southerly wind would begin to moderate after two o'clock, and her speed to slacken with it. She would haul up another point after passing the Highland, making a northwest, one half north, course, and logging a possible three miles and a half against a half-knot current. This would bring her at three o'clock two miles and a half off the beach at Truro, with High Head bearing southwest, one half west, three miles off.

Here she would be thirty-six miles by water to the north of her position on the Shoals at three o'clock on the day before, twenty-four hours earlier, but she had actually sailed through the water a distance of forty-seven and a half miles to get there, if she followed roughly the track I have outlined.

After three o'clock in the afternoon the wind would be dying down with the sun, but holding to the northwest, one half north, course, all sails would be drawing in good shape, and the *Mayflower* would at last be running out of the head tide she had held since daybreak. During the ebb slack, between three and four o'clock, she might make a couple of miles more of northing, which would place her at four o'clock with Peaked Hill Coast Guard Station bearing southwest by west, three and a half miles distant, the water twenty fathoms deep, and the sun only thirty-five minutes high.

At this point, the twenty-fathom curve, which he had been following all day at a distance of about two and a half or three miles off the beach, makes an abrupt bend in westerly toward the land, and unless Captain Jones hauled up sharp to a west course he would find himself stepping right off into twenty-five or thirty fathoms of water in short order. Although the wind was no doubt moderating fast as the sun drew down to the dunes, it was right offshore, the weather was fine and clear, and a making fair tide of a half-knot was pushing him where he wanted to go, and into deeper water all the time. Under these circumstances, and being reasonably sure from the descriptions of Gosnold and Captain John Smith, as well as from the personal experience of at least one of his Mates, Mr. Coppin, that there was plenty of bold water ahead, I firmly believe that he would haul her in and follow the edge as long as the daylight lasted, so as to get the lay of the land as much as possible before night shut down.

Logging a mile and a half an hour, and with a half-knot tide in his favor, when the sun set at four-thirty-five he would be just about where the Peaked Hill Bars Whistling Buoy is now located (1930), two and a half miles off the beach back of East Harbor, and with Peaked Hill Coast Guard Station bearing southwest, one half west, three miles distant. From this position, the Pilgrims on the deck of the *Mayflower* would see the sun set behind the hills where three centuries later the monument to their memory would rear its shaft. High Pole Hill, where the Pilgrim Monument is located, is very nearly five miles distant, southwest, one quarter west, from the Whistling Buoy, and ranges almost over Peaked Hill, where the Coast Guard Station is located.

By five o'clock, Peaked Hill would be south southwest, one half west, two miles distant, looming dimly against the afterglow; the wind would be light and off the land, and the tide would be sweeping the ship up toward the tip of the Cape almost a mile an hour, and into deeper water all the time. Captain Jones must have watched the sun go down on the night of Friday the tenth with much less misgiving than he did on the night before, when he had just clawed off from among the breakers of Pollack Rip Shoals, and had no idea of what lay ahead.

He had Race Point, which is the northern extremity of Cape Cod, in plain sight before dark. He had plenty of opportunity to observe both the speed of his ship and the set and velocity of the tidal current. He knew that he had plenty of water under his lee and ahead, and all he had to do, as long as it remained clear, was to shape a course to clear the Race, and let her jog until he was sure he was well out by it. He would not even consider anchoring in this location, where he could carry twenty fathoms of water right up into the beach grass.

Thus end the daylight hours of Friday the tenth of November, the second day for the Pilgrims on the American coast.

During the night of the tenth, off the Head of the Cape, the tactics of the navigating officer of the *Mayflower* would be essentially different from those of the night before, when he was keeping hold of the twenty-fathom edge to the northeast of Pollack Rip Shoals. Here, from Peaked Hill Bars clear around into Provincetown, there is plenty of water almost anywhere a mile off from the shore; and about all there was to it was to make sure he was out clear of the land in good shape, and then reach off and on till daylight. There was no twenty-fathom edge to keep tabs by, and he would have to look out not to get close enough in to poke his bowsprit into a sand dune. Aside from the fact that he would not want to stand off far enough to be out of sight of land at daybreak, there was comparatively little to worry about as long as the weather continued clear and comfortable.

As on the night before, it is altogether likely that Captain Jones held very light southerly airs through the night, the weather being in a mild and settled condition. There is no question but that it continued clear, and that the white beach knolls of the Race would be visible for quite a while after dark, and even by starlight and the light of the small moon during the latter half of the night, if he got very close in. At dark he would know his ship was logging about a mile an hour through the water and that the tide was giving him another mile, so, with the Race less than five miles distant, a three hours run making six miles good on a west course would carry him out by it handsomely.

As he neared Race Point, the tide would strengthen considerably, but after sunset the wind would undoubtedly lessen, and whether it did or not, he would put her under easy sail and slow her down as it grew darker, just keeping steerage way on her and logging perhaps a mile an hour through the night. Therefore, figuring a mile logged, and a knot fair tide an hour up to eight o'clock, would put him into thirty-two fathoms of water, with the Race bearing southeast, one half south, two miles and a quarter distant. It would have been possible to see the loom of the land abeam up to seven o'clock, about which time he would have been out by it and lost it in the gloom. Anyhow, his three hours' sailing time since five o'clock would tell him that by eight he was well out by, and ready to jog off and on until daylight hove up.

At eight o'clock, being sure he was well clear of the land, he would haul his ship sharp up by the wind, which would probably be south, or a little west of south, and very light. Under easy sail, close-hauled on the port tack, heading about west-south-west, and logging a mile an hour through the water, he would let her go offshore until twelve o'clock midnight.[40] He would hold a knot and a half tide right astern for the first hour, slacking to one knot after nine o'clock, but pushing him more to windward as he ranged in by the Race. Between nine-thirty and ten he would run into the high-water slack, having made good about four miles and a half on a southwest course, bringing him at ten o'clock into thirty fathoms of water and the Race bearing east northeast, four and a half miles distant.

Still letting her jog offshore, he would take the head tide, making in about a north by east direction, on his weather bow, running about a knot an hour from ten to eleven, and increasing to a knot and a half from eleven to twelve. Being close-hauled on the port tack, he would sag off across this tide, making a north-north-west course for a mile or so, giving him a position at twelve o'clock midnight of the tenth in thirty fathoms of water, with Race Point distant four miles and a half, bearing east by north.

Although he has not seen the land since seven o'clock the evening before, he has reached offshore for four hours or more since he cleared it, and it will now be safe to haul around on the starboard tack and head her in toward the land for a couple of hours, or half as long as he has headed off, and at the same speed. On this tack the ship heads about east-south-east, but, with a north-north-east tide of at least a knot and a half an hour sweeping her, broadside-to, to leeward, he makes a real course of east-north-east for three miles during the next two hours, which brings him at two o'clock of Saturday morning the eleventh, with Race Point bearing east by south, one half south, a mile and three quarters distant, in twenty-eight fathoms of water.

The moon rose about one-ten, and with it an hour high, even though it is small, on a clear starlit night the loom of the Race can be seen from this distance; and even if the Captain did not sight it, he would now tack offshore again for safety, having stood in half as long as he previously stood off, and having no definite information to go by as to the sweep of the tidal currents, nor the trend of the coastline here.

So at two o'clock he hauls her off on to the port tack again for two hours, heading west-south-west and taking the knot and a half north-north-east current on his weather bow, making good a course of north-north-west and sagging crab-fashion off across the tide for a mile.

At four o'clock he is back into thirty fathoms of water, the Race southeast by east, one half east, two miles and a half away, although perhaps not visible, daylight only two hours off, the moon three hours high, and the ebb or head tide slacking for the turn. Since the last turn of the tide he has lost about four or five miles of ground, but from now on the tide will be favorable until after ten o'clock in the forenoon.

He knows he can now safely stand in toward the land for two hours, which will take him up to six o'clock and daylight. By that time it will be light enough to see the land, and with the lead going and a sharp lookout, there will be little danger of running up on to the beach without warning, in the mean time. He hauls back on to the starboard tack, heading about east-south-east or better, with a southwest tide of a knot an hour pushing him to windward, and giving him a true course of southeast by south, one half south.

By five o'clock he can make out the Race, about a mile east on the port beam. Between five and six the tide increases to a knot and a half; and by six A.M., with daylight whitening the eastern sky and the dunes of the Cape looming spectral against it in the moonlight, he has made four miles and a half and gets into twenty-four fathoms of water, with the Race bearing north one half east, two and three quarters miles distant, and Wood End a mile and three quarters east by south.

After six o'clock, as he works in by Wood End, still close hauled on the starboard tack and heading east-south-east by the compass, the tide follows more and more astern, setting about south-south-east a knot an hour, and giving him a southeast course for two miles during the next hour.

The sun comes up red and clear from behind the Truro hills about 6:55 A.M., and at seven he has Wood End bearing north-north-east, a mile and a quarter distant, the water shoaling from twenty fathoms, broad daylight and a fair tide to take him into the Harbor. He can now swing the *Mayflower* off to due east for a mile and a half, with the half knot flood pushing him right along on his course, and the wind free.

If the wind came up with the sun, as it customarily does, he would clew up his mainsails and foresails and snug her down so that he could feel his way along slowly into the harbor with the hand-lead. By eight he would be into fifteen fathoms of water, with Long Point, the tip of the arm which encircles Provincetown Harbor, bearing north by east, a mile and a half distant, Pamet River in sight across the Bay four miles to the east-south-east, and the water getting shoaler rapidly.

At eight o'clock he swings her off to northeast by north, one half north, for the Harbor, sounding in through the best of the water and carrying fifteen fathoms or better, for a mile and three quarters, which brings him at nine o'clock with Long Point due west, and half a mile distant.

Here the water shoals up into ten fathoms, so he gybes over and hauls up sharply to the westward for the inner harbor, which is now opening up in plain sight. Finding nothing but soft mud and poor holding ground in the middle of the Harbor, with shoals and flats all along the northerly and westerly sides under the mainland, he finally stands back on to the hard bottom under the lee of the Point.

At ten o'clock in the forenoon of Saturday, the eleventh of November, 1620, O.S., just as four bells chimes out from the ship's belfry on the break of the half-deck, Master Christopher Jones shoots his ship into the wind and lets go his anchor in twelve fathoms of water, about an eighth of a mile inside of Long Point; and the *Mayflower* of London, sixty-seven days out from Plymouth, England, swings to her moorings in the New World.

If Captain Jones worked half as hard in bringing the *Mayflower* around into Provincetown from the time he first made the land at Nauset as I have, he had not spent much time in his bunk for the last forty-eight hours. I sincerely hope he could now turn his ship over to a Master's Mate to put a harbor furl into her sails, and go below for a much-needed sleep.

It may seem to the landsman that I have run the *Mayflower* up from the Shoals and around into Provincetown in a rather nonchalant manner, so to speak. This is not the case, by any manner of means. Every mile, on every course, for every hour, has been carefully estimated in relation to the known capabilities of the *Mayflower,* the known tidal currents which obtained during the period she was making the passage, and the weather conditions which it seems certain she encountered.

While there is no landmark given nor hour mentioned in any record known to me, giving any clue to her whereabouts on Friday the tenth, there are certain conditions which must be accepted. The most important is that without a fair wind she could not have made the run up the Back Side of the Cape at all, nor any part of it, as any sailor will concede. The second is that no shipmaster in his sound senses would attempt to run very far in the darkness of night, on this extremely dangerous coast, in the circumstances in which Captain Jones found himself.

With these facts accepted as a basis, we have eleven hours of daylight sailing for the tenth, and less than half of that for the forenoon of the eleventh, in which to cover the fifty miles of water between the Shoals and the anchorage at Provincetown. At the most liberal estimate we cannot get more than sixteen to eighteen hours of daylight out of it, and it is certain the *Mayflower* covered at least seventy-five miles of actual mileage to make it. Her best speed that we know of was not much over four miles an hour, and at this rate she would need nearly eighteen hours to cover the distance, with a good stiff breeze much of the time, at that.

I have rated her day's work of the tenth on those conditions, and while every position may not be exact to a mile, the whole trip must be approximately correct, and the hourly average nearly so. A ship of 1620 conformed to the unwritten rules of the sea just as closely as a ship of 1930, and a skillful commander of that period held to the same line of reasoning as the modern shipmaster of today. The only essential differences are in the data at hand on which to base decisions and the physical limitations of the ship herself. It has been my aim, in every possible way, to navigate the *Mayflower* from the perspective of the handicaps under which Captain Jones labored, and to meet the natural conditions of shoals, weather, and tides, from that standpoint.

As to the direction of the wind on the morning of Saturday the eleventh, it makes very little difference what quarter it was from. In working into Provincetown Harbor a ship heads to every point of the compass, 'boxes the compass,' as a sailor expresses it. A fair wind in one place is a head wind in another, and the *Mayflower* could work in on the flood tide, which it is certain she held until nearly noon, no matter where the wind was from.

It is absolutely certain, however, that she never could have got up around the Head of the Cape far enough to slip into Provincetown on the morning of the eleventh, unless she had held a fair, southerly wind all day of the tenth, and it would be likely to breeze up from the same quarter again the next morning, and hold until the turn of the tide, at least. Therefore, I have given her the benefit of this probability.

That the *Mayflower* never stood far out into the Bay away from the Head of the Cape by daylight is certain, or she would have sighted the high hills of Manomet on the Plymouth shore, which were less than fifteen miles distant. With a southerly wind it is likely to be more or less hazy, and no doubt the visibility was not as good as on the morning she first sighted land. Had they seen this headland, it is very probable they would have mentioned it, just as they did the mouth of Pamet, 'opening itself into the mainland,' which they saw as they 'sailed into the harbour.'[11] That Pamet appeared to be 'some 2 or 3 leagues of'—that is, over six miles distant—supports the probability that they were hugging the Provincetown shore pretty closely, because in reality Pamet is only four and a half miles from Long Point itself, and at most not over four miles from any conceivable position they could have been in. That it did appear to be at such a distance also tends to the belief that they ran into the Harbor with a southerly wind, for, if they had had to tack back and forth against a head wind in order to get in, they must, perforce, have stood across toward the Truro shore, and brought Pamet near enough not to warrant any such appearance. That they saw it plainly enough to suppose that it was an opening into the mainland shows that the weather still held comparatively clear.

The exact location of the *Mayflower*'s anchorage is definitely fixed by one of the passengers. In describing the start of the third exploring expedition, on the sixth of December, he says: 'wee were a long while after we launched from the ship, before we could get cleare of a sandie poynt, which lay within lesse then a furlong of the same.'[42] The English furlong was, and is, one eighth of a mile, or six hundred and sixty feet. Just this distance inside of Long Point today is a deep hole, carrying twelve fathoms of water almost to low-water mark,[43] the best holding ground and most sheltered anchorage in the Harbor. It was formerly much used for this purpose, but because of its distance from the village, which lies across the Harbor, it has fallen into disuse. It is still there as good as ever.

I have made some study as to the changes which may have taken place in and around Provincetown Harbor, in order that I might feel reasonably sure where to anchor the *Mayflower*. The results have been interesting and illuminating, but as this is not the place for a discussion of this research, except as it affects the place where the *Mayflower* lay, I shall confine myself to that locality. Contrary to what might be supposed, the tendency seems to be for Long Point to build *up*, but not *out*. In fact, since 1848, there is authentic proof that the actual shoreline above low-water mark has receded by a very little.[44] So far as I have learned, nothing has happened to alter appreciably the little pothole of anchorage where the *Mayflower* lay, nor the relative distance of the tip of the Point from it.

In order to check up on ten o'clock as the approximate hour at which the *Mayflower* came to anchor, we have the record of the happenings of the eleventh to help. Both Bradford and Mourt's Relation agree that the Compact was drawn up and signed on the morning of the eleventh. The Relation puts it thus: 'This day before we came to harbour, observing some not well affected to unitie and concord...it was thought good there should be an association and agreement, that we should combine together in one body...and set our hands to this that follows word for word.'[45]

Bradford, describing the same occurrence, says: 'a combination made by them before they came ashore.'[46] From this evidence it is clear that this memorable document was drawn up and signed, not only before they sent any landing party ashore, but even before they dropped anchor in the Harbor—'before we came to harbour,' to refer back to the exact words of the men who signed it. Evidently the leaders among the Pilgrims took no chances whatever that any disaffected members of their company should get away from the ship and on to dry land until they had agreed to abide by the decisions of the majority, they being out of all jurisdiction granted in their English charter, and wholly dependent on their own initiative to regulate the body politic.

The date of the Compact, the eleventh of November,[47] makes it certain that it was signed on the morning when they 'came to harbour.' It is reasonable to assume that the men would not be assembled to sign this far-reaching agreement until daylight, nor until after breakfast was out of the way. It is not likely that breakfast was finished before seven-thirty or eight o'clock, and it is reasonable to suppose that it might take twenty-one men at least a half or three quarters of an hour to set their names to paper, one after another. Writing was a laborious undertaking in those days, and took time, even if some could no more than make their marks. Two or three minutes to a man may not be too much to allow, before each one had walked up to the table, written his signature, or had it written for him and made his mark, and made way for the next signer.

It might well be nine o'clock before the last man had signed, and 'they came to harbor,' which would leave only an hour before I calculate the *Mayflower* cast her anchor. This hour would be needed in which to choose a landing party and make them ready to go ashore.

They tell us that

> the same day so soon as we could we set ashore 15. or 16. men, well armed, with some to fetch wood, for we had none left; as also to see what the Land was, and what Inhabitants they could meet with, they found it to be a small neck of Land; on this side where we lay is the Bay, and the further side the Sea; the ground or earth, sand hils, much like the Downes in Holland, but much better; the crust of the earth a Spits depth, excellent blacke earth; all wooded with Okes, Pines, Sassafras, Juniper, Birch, Holly, Vines, some Ash, Walnut; the wood for the most part open and without under-wood, fit either to goe or ride in: at night our people returned, but found not any person, nor habitation, and laded their Boat with Juniper, which smelled very sweet & strong, and of which we burnt the most part of the time we lay there.[48]

From this description there is no question whatever as to which side of the Harbor they made this landing on. There is not the remotest evidence to show that either then or since has Long Point, near where the *Mayflower* lay, ever boasted such a growth of vegetation as they saw, nor a crust of earth of a 'Spits depth,'[49] and, furthermore, they had had plenty of opportunity to see all the topography of this stretch of sand as they came in around it. From the maintop lookout of the *Mayflower*, and almost from her poop deck, they could have seen every clump of beach grass from Wood End to the Channel, and no 'Inhabitant' nor 'habitation' could have escaped their ken. Allowing for a possible washing away of the shorefront, and a drifting in of sand over old forest growths on the westerly side of the Harbor, does not alter materially the relative configuration of the shores.

With a landing party ready to go ashore as soon as the ship came to anchor, it would take the better part of an hour to get the ship's longboat over the side, embark the men, their arms and axes, and row across the Harbor a mile or more to the northern shore. The logical place to expect them to land would be on the point which is now represented by the southern extremity of the town. Here they would carry deep water in toward the shore farther than anywhere else, and, in addition, be least exposed to a sudden attack by any savages who might be lurking to give them a hot reception.

They tell us that they were 'forced to wade a bowshoot or two in going a-land';[50] and this would be only too true. The longboat was a heavy craft, probably twenty-two feet long by seven wide, at least, and with fifteen or sixteen men, loaded down with matchlocks and armor, besides a squad of wood-choppers with their tools, she could not have drawn much less than two or three feet of water. The tide was high about eleven o'clock that day in Provincetown Harbor, but by noon it would be on the ebb, which would add to their difficulties. I do not see how they could possibly have set foot on dry land much before high noon, giving due consideration to what they had already accomplished since daylight.

Figure 6. The Pilgrim's First Landing Place. Provincetown, Massachusetts

After landing, they explored the surrounding country sufficiently to bring back a description so minutely detailed as to answer almost as well today. They must have scouted far enough to have gained the top of High Pole Hill, where the monument stands today, in order to have seen the sea on the 'further side' of the Cape. In the mean time they had accumulated a supply of juniper, and of course lugged it off on their backs, through water knee-deep, to the longboat, which in itself is no slouch of a job, with the boat a 'bowshoot or two' from the shore, and the wood certainly some distance above high-water mark.

All this took time; and that they did it all and returned to the ship 'att dark,' which would shut down soon after sunset at four-thirty-five, must argue strongly for a period of at least four or five hours on the land. Therefore, it is reasonable to suppose that the result of my previous calculations, which brought the *Mayflower* to anchor about ten o'clock in the forenoon of Saturday the eleventh of November, 1620, O.S., must be approximately correct.

Although I have tried my best to condense this narrative, I fear I have tired my readers with all these soundings and bearings and courses, which to most must read like so much Greek. It has seemed to me necessary, however, to say about what I have said, in order to make each conclusion clear, as it appears to me. If the telling has been long, what must the actual days have been to our Pilgrim fathers and mothers, huddled in a cold, bilgy ship, without firewood, short of water, with the wintry blasts whistling through the rigging, and no homes to welcome them when at last they made the Harbor!

As for myself, I have enjoyed every minute I have spent as shipmates with the *Mayflower*, and it is almost with a feeling of regret that I pack my clothes-bag and get my discharge-papers, as it were, from the good old ship. There seemed so little from which to work, when I first started out to attempt to unravel the story of the days she spent off back of the Cape, that it hardly seemed possible ever to get anywhere near a solution. As I have worked along from milestone to milestone, however, it has unfolded logically and systematically, so that each hour has held its own little surprise of satisfaction. Information has come to me from such wholly unexpected sources, and in such volume, that I feel I have really been rather fortunate, and the contacts I have made through my search for data have been a source of pleasure.

Perhaps there are some, who, like myself, will stand on Nauset Beach and think that, off there at daybreak, the *Mayflower* once crept slowly in toward the Back Side for the first time; or gazing south at sunset from Chatham Light, on James's Head, picture brave Captain Jones conning his ship unerringly out from among the sinister Shoals, which have pounded so many good ships to their doom.

It is all very real to me. I can, in fancy, hear the gurgle of her cutwater, as the *Mayflower* cautiously rounds in by Long Point on that chill November morning three hundred years ago. I hear the hiss of her main-cable as her anchor gratefully tastes the waters of a New World, the mud of the Old still sticking to its flukes. Here I will leave her, gently swinging to her moorings on the blue waters of the Bay, her Pilgrim passengers giving thanks to their Living God for bringing them safely across the 'vast and furious ocean,' the while they grimly trim their matchlocks for the work ahead.

THE END

Notes

1. Mourt, 1, 2. [vpon the ninth of Nouember following, by breake of the day we efpied land which we deemed to be *Cape Cod*, and fo afterward it proued.]
2. Bradford, 93. [litle]
3. *Ibid.*, 93.
4. *Ibid.*, 97.
5. Introduction to Mourt, xvii.
6. Mourt, 3, 5-7; Bradford, 97, 109, 110.
7. Mourt, 11, 12.
8. The Naval Observatory, Washington, D. C., informs me that this is the difference between July and November.
9. Bradford, 93. [faire]
10. When Bradford wrote his *History*, he had not only made the passage over on the *Mayflower*, but had made several coastal voyages on his own account since that time.
11. Calculation by the Naval Observatory, Washington, D. C.
12. It was full moon October 30. *Ibid.*
13. Captain T. Carroll Nickerson, of East Harwich.
14. Captain George B. Nickerson, Nauset Coast Guard.
15. The sun rose about 6:55 A.M., November 9, 1620, O.S. The moon rose about eleven-thirty the evening before. Naval Observatory calculations, within a few minutes.
16. The old moon rises with its horns to the west. The new moon sets with its horns to the east.
17. Bradford, 93.
18. *Ibid.*
19. Mourt, 2, 3. [wee made our courfe South South Weft, purpofing to goe to a Riuer ten leagues to the South of the Cape, but at night the winde being contrary, we put round againe for the Bay of *Cape Cod.*]
20. In spite of Dexter's suggestion (Mourt, p. 2, note 5) that 'An error of the press for south-south-*east* is not improbable,' I must say, and stick to it, that there is no chance that there was an error of the press. I fully realize the futility of my taking exceptions to such an authority, but it is evident that Dexter had in mind that the *Mayflower* was somewhere off the Head of the Cape: that is, in the neighborhood of where Highland Light stands today, when she made the land. In that case, a south-south-*west* course would soon have 'brought them directly on the cape,' as Dexter says. A careful reading of the following pages of my paper, however, will show that she could not have been much over twenty-one miles to the north of the Shoals of Pollack Rip when she tacked ship and started on her southerly course. This places her about off the Eastham shore, from which a south-south-*west* course is the only correct one to the Shoals. Even had she been where Dexter and others place her, a south-south-*east* course, as he suggests, would have been about as seriously in error as a south-south-*west*, because by the *Mayflower*'s compass, which in 1620 showed a west declination

of more than thirteen degrees, a south-south-*east* course would have taken her out of sight of land before she ever got down to Chatham, and she would never have become entangled with the Shoals of Pollack Rip, nor any others, until she fetched up somewhere down around the Capes of South America. Although I have the greatest respect for the opinions of Dexter as an historian, the facts are as I have stated.

21. Naval Observatory, Washington, D.C., calculation, for ninth November, 1620, O.S.
22. Bradford, 93.
23. Mourt, 2, 3.
24. The depths shown in feet on the map are from the Coast and Geodetic Survey.
25. Direction and velocity of tide, from Captain Tobin, Pollack Lightship 110.
26. An experienced pilot in these waters puts it this way: 'The Pilgrims never knew how near they came to settling on Monomoy Point.'
27. Any sailor familiar with the Shoals will see by glancing at the chart that this course, right before wind and tide, would shove her five or six miles out toward the twenty-fathom edge, in an hour's time.
28. The moon rose about 12:20 A.M. November 10, 1620, O.S. Naval Observatory calculation.
29. It was four days before new moon, which gives high water here at about eight-forty to nine. The Naval Observatory at Washington has confirmed this calculation. The velocities and directions of the currents I have obtained from the Coast and Geodetic Survey, fishermen, coast guardsmen, lightship men, pilots, and so on.
30. Special emphasis is laid on the fact that after the arrival of the *Mayflower* in Provincetown Harbor, during the time of the exploring expeditions, the weather became boisterous and wintry, a change from what they had experienced. See Bradford, 101, and Mourt, 27.
31. All heights of land are from the Topographic Maps of the United States Geological Survey.
32. The Highland can be seen for more than fifteen miles offshore in clear weather.
33. Mourt, 2.
34. Bradford, 93. [fell with that land which is called Cape Cod; the which being made & certainly knowne to be it, they were not a litle joyfull.]
35. There is a bare possibility that Stephen Hopkins had been to America once before, and perhaps some of the Pilgrim company's hired seamen. See Vol. III, *History of North America*, by Guy Carleton Lee. [74]
36. Clark and Coppin.
37. Mourt, 12: 'Our women to wash, as they had great need,' were landed as soon as possible in Provincetown, showing the scarcity of fresh water aboardship. [our women to waſh, as they had great need;]
38. Mourt, 8, 9: 'some to fetch wood, for we had none left.' This was the very day they arrived at Provincetown. [ſome to fetch wood, for we had none left.]
39. The soundings given are the depths at mean low water, as given on the latest

Coast and Geodetic Survey charts. The bearings and courses are given in 'points,' rather than in degrees, and are corrected to the magnetic compass bearings of 1620 as nearly as possible. The direction and velocity of tidal currents are based on the Current Tables for different stations as published by the Department of Commerce, and corrected to the different positions of the ship and the period of the tide.

40. An interesting comment by an experienced pilot, Captain Francis E. Hammond, who has sailed these waters for over twenty-five years, may be of interest. In checking over my calculations, he made this note: 'It is nineteen miles from Highland Light to the Steamboat Dock in Provincetown—and of course the *Mayflower* would make it a great deal farther. This is just half as far as it is from the Highland to Boston Light. If the old boy [meaning the captain of the *Mayflower*] had stood across the Bay, instead of trying to get around into Provincetown, he could have been in Boston Harbor before he could have got into Provincetown.'

   Headed for Boston, he would have held a fair tide, or practically none at all against him, and with a southerly wind would have been well across before daylight, instead of being in almost the same location at daylight that he was the night before. But he did not know that.

41. Mourt, 13. Bradford, 97-98, says: 'as they wente into yt harbor ther seemed to be an opening some 2 or 3 leagues of.' [Mourt: opening it felfe into the maine land; Bradford: 2.]

42. Mourt, 45. [wee were a long while after we launched from the fhip, before we could get cleare of a fandie poynt, which lay within leffe then a furlong of the fame.]

43. See Coast and Geodetic Survey Chart 341.

44. A comparison of the surveys made by the Coast and Geodetic Survey since that date, and kindly furnished me by that Department, proves this. I have also studied the Harbor Commissioner's Reports, the Reports of the Province Lands Legislative committees, etc., and compared my findings with old maps and charts, with the same results.

45. Mourt, 5-6. [This day before we came to harbour, obferuing fome not well affected to vnitie and concord...it was thought good there fhould be an affociation and agreement, that we fhould combine together in one body...and fet our hands to this that followes word for word.]

46. Bradford, 109.

47. Mourt, 7; Bradford, 110.

48. Mourt, 8-11. [The fame day fo foon as we could we fet a-fhore 15. or 16. men, well armed, with fome to fetch wood, for we had none left; as alfo to fee what the Land was, and what Inhabitants they could meet with, they found it to be a fmall neck of Land; on this fide where we lay is the Bay, and the further fide of the Sea; the ground or earth, fand hils, much like the Downes in *Holland*, but much better; the cruft of the earth a Spits depth, excellent blacke earth; all wooded with Okes, Pines, Saffafras, Iuniper, Birch, Holly, Vines, fome Afh,

Walnut; the wood for the moſt part open and without vnder-wood, fit either to goe or ride in: at night our people returned, but found not any perſon, nor habitation, and laded their Boat with Iuniper, which ſmelled very ſweet & ſtrong, and of which we burnt the moſt part of the time we lay there.]

49. A spade's depth. Some eminent authorities claim that Long Point was the landing-place, both for this party and for the women who landed to do their washing. The women were looking for *fresh* water, I can assure you—they had had plenty of *salt* for the last two months—and the only place to find this was on the north side of the Harbor.

50. Mourt, 5; See also Mourt, 27. [forced to wade a bow ſhoot or two in going a-land,]

Bibliography

Ancient Maps in the collections of the Massachusetts Historical Society, Boston Athenaeum, Boston Public Library, State Street Trust Company, and Private Collections.

Anderson, R. C. "A 'Mayflower' Model." *The Mariners' Mirror.* 12 (1926): 260-63.

Archer, Gabriel and John Brereton. *The Gosnold Discoveries. . . in the North Part of Virginia, 1602 Now Cape Cod and the Islands, Massachusetts.* Edited by Lincoln A. Dexter. Sturbridge: Plaza Printing, 1982.

Blunt, Edmund M. *The American Coast Pilot Containing Directions for the Principal Harbors, Capes and Headlands of the Coast of North and South America.* New York: E. G. N. Blunt, 1854.

Bowman, George Ernest. "The Will of William Mullins." *The* Mayflower *Descendant.* 1 (1899): 230-31.

Bowditch, Nathaniel. *American Practical Navigator, an Epitome of Navigation.* Washington: Department of Defense, Defense Mapping Agency Hydrographic Center, 1 (1977); 2 (1975).

Bowditch, N. I. *Memoir of Nathaniel Bowditch.* Cambridge, 1884.

Bradford, William. *Bradford's History "Of Plimoth Plantation."* Boston: Wright and Potter Printing Co., State Printers, 1899.

Chatterton, E. Keble. *Sailing Ships and Their Story.* Philadelphia: J. B. Lippincott Co., 1923.

Commonwealth of Massachusetts. Report of Commissioners on Cape Cod and East Harbors, 5 Jan. 1853. Senate No. 6 and 16 Jan. 1854. Senate No. 5.

Daniel, Hawthorne. *Ships of the Seven Seas.* Garden City: New York: Doubleday, Page & Co., 1925.

Davis, William T. *Ancient Landmarks of Plymouth.* Boston: Damrell and Upham, 1899.

DeCosta, B. F. *Cavo de Baros, or the Place of Cape Cod in the Old Cartography.* New York, 1881.

Dexter, Henry Martyn, ed. *Mourt's Relation or Journal of the Plantation at Plymouth.* Boston: John Kimball Wiggin, 1865.

Dexter, Henry Martyn and Morton Dexter. *The England and Holland of the Pilgrims.* Boston and New York: Houghton, Mifflin and Co. Cambridge: The Riverside Press, 1905.

Deyo, Simeon L., ed. *History of Barnstable County, Mass.* New York, 1890.

Eldridge, George and George W. Eldridge. *Eldridge's Coast Pilot No. 4, From New York to Boston.* Boston: George W. Eldridge, 1893.

Forbes, Allan and Paul F. Cadman. *France and New England.* Issued by State Street Trust Company of Boston, Publication 3. Boston: Walton Advertising & Printing Co., 1929.

Freeman, Frederick. *The History of Cape Cod: The Annals of Barnstable County and its Several Towns.* 2 vols. Yarmouth Port: Parnassus Imprints, 1965.

Freeman, James. *A Description of the East Coast of Cape Cod.* Boston, 1802.

Gorges, Fernando. "Brief Narration of the Original Undertakings of the Advancement of Plantations into the Parts of America . . ." In Maine Historical Society *Collections,* 1st ser. 2 (1847), 1-65 (2nd pagination).

Grant, W. L., ed. *Voyages of Samuel de Champlain 1604-1618.* New York: Charles Scribner's Sons, 1907.

Hakluyt, Richard E. *Discourse of Western Planting.* Edited by David B. Quinn and Alison M. Quinn. London: Hakluyt Society, 1993.

Henderson, William James. *The Elements of Navigation.* New York: Harper & Bros., 1917.

Holmes, George Charles Vincent. *Ancient and Modern Ships—Part I Wooden Sailing Ships.* Covent Garden: Chapman & Hall, 1900.

Hutchinson, J. R. "The *Mayflower,* Her Identity and Tonnage." *The New England Historical and Genealogical Register.* 70:337-42. Boston: The Society, 1916.

Josselyn, John. *An Account of Two Voyages to New-England, Made during the Years 1638, 1663.* Boston: William Veazie, 1865. The original title page: *Chronological Observations of America to 1673.* London: Giles Widdowes, 1674.

Juet, Robert. *Juet's Journal. The Voyage of the Half Moon from 4 April to 7 November 1609.* Edited by Robert M. Lunny. The Collections of the New Jersey Historical Society 12:16-19. Newark: The New Jersey Historical Society, 1959.

Records of the Colony of New Plymouth in New England. Edited by David Pulsifer. Vol. 1, 1620-1651. Boston: Press of William White, 1861.

Kittredge, Henry C. *Cape Cod Its People and Their History.* 2d ed. With a Post-Epilogue by John Hay, 1930-1968. Orleans: Parnassus Imprints, Inc., 1968.

Lechford, Thomas. *Note-Book Kept by Thomas Lechford, Esq., Lawyer, in Boston, Massachusetts Bay, from June 27, 1638 to July 29, 1641.* Cambridge: John Wilson and Son. University Press, 1885.

Lee, Guy Carleton, ed. *The History of North America Volume Three The Colonization of the South by Peter Joseph Hamilton.* Philadelphia: George Barrie & Sons, 1904.

Livermore, Charles W. and Leander Crosby. *The Ancient Wreck, Loss of the Sparrow-Hawk in 1626. Remarkable Preservation and Recent Discovery of the Wreck.* (Anonymous pamphlet.) Boston: Alfred Mudge and Son, 1865.

Local Information about the Back Side of Cape Cod from Coast Guard Captains, Lightship Masters, Captains of fishermen, Master Pilots, and a host of other men.

Marsden, R. G. "The *Mayflower.*" The Mayflower *Descendant* 18 (1916): 1-13.

Mitchell, Henry. Article and Charts on Monomoy. U.S. Coast and Geodetic Survey, 1886.

Moriarty, G. Andrews Jr. "Notes." *The New England Historical and Genealogical Register* 83:250-51. Boston: The Society, 1929.

Morison, Samuel Eliot. *The Maritime History of Massachusetts 1783-1860.* Boston and New York: Houghton Mifflin Co. Cambridge: The Riverside Press, 1921.

Morton, Nathaniel. *New England's Memorial.* Boston: Crocker and Brewster, 1826.

Otis, Amos. "An Account of the Discovery of an Ancient Ship on the Eastern Shore of Cape Cod." *The New England Historical and Genealogical Register* 18:37-44. Albany: J. Munsell, 1864.

Paine, Josiah. *A History of Harwich Barnstable County Massachusetts 1620-1800 Including The Early History of That Part Now Brewster, With Some Account of its Indian Inhabitants.* Yarmouthport, Massachusetts: Parnassus Imprints, 1971.

Plymouth Colony, Barnstable County, and Cape Cod Town Records.

Pratt, Rev. Enoch. *A Comprehensive History, Ecclesiastical and Civil, of Eastham, Wellfleet and Orleans, County of Barnstable, Mass. From 1644 to 1844.* Yarmouth: W. S. Fisher and Co., 1844.

Purchas, Samuel. *Purchas, His Pilgrimage or, Relations of the World and the Religions Observed in All Ages.* London: William Stansby, 1626.

Report of Committee on Cape Cod Harbor, 1857. Public Document No. 36.

Rich, Shebnah. *Truro, Cape Cod, or Land Marks and Sea Marks.* Boston: D. Lothrop, 1884.

Senate Report on Condition of Province Lands, January 1838. Senate No. 6.

Shaler, Nathaniel. *Geology of the Cape District* from 18th Annual Report of U. S. Geological Survey, 1896-97.

Ship Models in National Museum, Washington, D.C.; Commercial Museum, Philadelphia; Museum of Science and Industry, Chicago; Pilgrim Museum, Plymouth; Peabody Museum, Salem; Old State House, Boston; Old Dartmouth Historical Society, New Bedford; State Street Trust Company, Boston; Boston Marine Society, Boston; and other privately owned models.

Slafter, Edmund F., ed. *Voyages of Samuel De Champlain.* Vol. 2 (1604-1610). Boston: The Prince Society, 1878.

Smith, Captain John. *A Description of New England; or, Observations and Discoveries in the North of America in the Year of Our Lord 1614.* Boston: William Veazie, 1865.

Smith, Stanley W. "Records of the First Church in Orleans, Formerly the First Church in Eastham, Mass." *The* Mayflower *Descendant* 14 (1912): 53-56.

Smith, William C. *A History of Chatham Massachusetts.* 4th ed. Chatham: The Chatham Historical Society, Inc., 1992.

Stratton, Eugene Aubrey. *Plymouth Colony—Its History and People 1620-1691.* Salt Lake City: Ancestry Publishing, 1986.

The Massachusetts Magazine. 3 (Jan. 1791): Map of Cape Cod and the Parts Adjacent is between pages 24-25.

Winslow, Edward. *Good News From New England, The Story of the Pilgrim Fathers, 1606-1623 A.D.; as told by Themselves, their Friends, and their Enemies.* Edited by Edward Arber. Boston: Houghton, Mifflin and Co., 1897.

Winsor, Justin. *Narrative and Critical History of America.* Vol. 1-Part II. Boston and New York: Houghton, Mifflin and Company. Cambridge: The Riverside Press, 1889.

————. *The Memorial History of Boston Including Suffolk County, Massachusetts 1630-1880, The Early and Colonial Periods.* Vol. 1. Boston: Ticknor & Co., 1880.

Winthrop, John. The History of New England from 1630 to 1649. 2 vols. Boston: Little, Brown and Co., 1853.

Wood, William. *New England's Prospect.* Edited by Alden T. Vaughan. Amherst: University of Massachusetts Press, 1977.

Young, Alexander, ed. *Chronicles of the Pilgrim Fathers of the Colony of Plymouth, from 1602 to 1625.* Boston: Charles C. Little and James Brown, 1841.

Index